My Help Cometh

Victoria Stith

ISBN 979-8-89243-510-9 (paperback)
ISBN 979-8-89243-511-6 (digital)

Christian Faith Publishing
832 Park Avenue
Meadville, PA 16335
www.christianfaithpublishing.com

Printed in the United States of America

Contents

Section 1

The Beginning

Genesis 1:26, Psalm 139:14, Isaiah 9:6 KJV

It took me into my fifties before I truly realized that my life, our lives, and your life are patterned after God. We as parents/caregivers are supposed to follow the example that God, our Heavenly Father, has set before us. It is God's promise, creation, and the proof of his appointed "prophets" that open my eye, giving me full hope, never giving up, and always, always having trust and faith in him.

In loving memory of William Arelus Mackey Jr., a.k.a
Bill Mackey, June Mackey, Uncle June, Junior

February 9, 1947 (sunrise) to December 30, 2022 (sunset)

Bill was loved by his children, grandchildren, great-children, family, and friends. If you hired him to do a job, from changing the locks on your door to carpentry and from plumbing to laying cement or putting up a fence in your backyard, he was honest, trustworthy, and would do the work he was hired for with pride and respect. We love him and miss him dearly. He left behind a lot of funny and loving memories.

Acknowledgments

I thank God for planting the seed of *My Help Cometh* inside me, giving me the courage to not just look at how I'm exposing myself but also be able to share my story, my life experiences, where I was, where I am today, and what God has in store for me.

Again, I always have to thank my family and friends. They mean so much to me; they pray for me, they support me, they give me wisdom and insight, and at times, they put the truth in my face, especially my daughters. A special thanks to my family, friends, coworkers, and church family who have purchased *Who Am I, I Am*.

Love always,
Victoria J. Stith

This picture was taken in 2021 at home.

Introduction

My Help Cometh is an invigorating autobiography centering on my life, my family, my education, my work, and most importantly, my love for Jesus Christ, my personal Lord and Savior, being able to bring to life my story of overcoming guilt, shame, addictions, my distortion of love, anger, and mental health issues. As I got clean, going to meetings, getting therapy, and attending church, I started telling my story verbally and through journal writing. My family and friends heard my testimonies, struggles, survivals, and accomplishments; more than just conversation, they saw that I could help and be a blessing to others who are going through what I've been through.

Stepping out of my comfort zone, exposing the real me, the phony, the not-so-popular me, there I am, drug-free and alcohol-free, yet facing head-on my failures, my faults, my trials, my tribulations, which helped me turn mere dreams into realities and at the same time keep my promise to God that no matter what I went through, I would never use drugs or alcohol again. Because of this bond between God and myself, I have managed to keep that promise from July 11, 1994, to this very day. And I'm so happy about that.

Fast-forwarding through a long process of recovery, renewing, and reviving my relationship with God, I realize today that God's plan continues to guide my life even when I fall short. I've learned to incorporate the twelve steps and the Ten Commandments; for me, I can't work one without the other. I know my boundaries, and I am no longer looking back at what I would've done, should've done, or could've done or been. My focus is on the present, planning my future of what I am and what I can be through prayer, support, and advice from my family and friends.

How he still opens up opportunities and situations that lead me to have sympathy toward others, especially for others who are different from me. Each day he gives me the guts to fight and to do what's right for myself, my family, and my community. I'm grateful for my mistakes because they are my learning tools. I must keep working daily to accept God's divine plan for me. From this, "my help definitely cometh from the Lord."

I will lift mine eyes unto the hills, from whence cometh my help. (Psalm 121:1 KJV)

Victoria J. Stith, a.k.a. Sister Stith, Grandma, Mom, Mizz Vickie, and Vickie

Prayer of Thanksgiving

The Lord is good. It is He, that made us,
not we ourselves. (Psalm 100:3–4 KJV)

Dear Father God,

Thank you, Father God, for giving me the courage to live again. You knew the kind of person I had become: rebellious, disobedient, and disrespectful to my parents and other adult figures. I turned away from the advice and wisdom that was my road to success in my young adulthood. I took you for granted, the wrong I did to my family, abandoning my own children so I could live a selfish, ungodly, destructive lifestyle. I stole, lied, and cheated for worldly pleasures. Despite my wicked ways, you saw something in me. You saw my heart and soul. You continued then and now to provide for me with your grace and mercy as your son, Jesus, protects and guides me in my life. I thank you for giving me back to my family, for giving me back my dignity and respect. I thank you for putting the most unlikely people in my life to mentor, sponsor, and minister to me in ways I could never imagine. When I'm feeling alone, you were and are there. When I couldn't and didn't see and conceive, you had a divine plan for me; you continue to give me the courage to use my past and present mistakes to help others and remind them they don't have to walk the wide path. They don't have to feel that life is over and they will never be forgiven. For this, I will always be eternally grateful to you, Father God.

Although this book is not about me, my prayer, Father God, is that everyone who reads this book will find the courage within them to change for the better. To accept your Son, Jesus, in their hearts and to ask you to fill them with the Holy Ghost. To look to you for help, especially in challenging times when the enemy creeps in to say, "People won't like you," "Your friends will turn their noses up to you," "You really don't need to say that because it's none of their business anyway." I will turn back to you and rebuke the devil who only wants to destroy me.

Your hands are stretched out all day and night for us to come to you. You let us know through the Holy Bible of forgiveness of oneself and others, followed by hope, by serving and loving one another unconditionally (Matthew 5:44 and Matthew 6:9–14 KJV). You give us examples each and every day of your unchanging love and mercy toward us. For this, I will always be eternally grateful to you. Forevermore in the name of your Son, Jesus. Amen.

Section 2

Personal Testimony

In the world, I was just a fleeting person, wandering aimlessly. Because of you, Father God, you protected me over and over again. "Fear thou not; for I am with thee: be not dismayed; for I am thy God: I will help thee; yea, I will uphold thee with the right hand of my righteousness" (Isaiah 41:10).

Dear Father God in heaven,

I thank you in the mighty, matchless name of your Son, Jesus, for always satisfying me in the times when I least expect.

Thank you for the food and drink you provide for my physical needs, but it's the spiritual food and drink that, from your hands, satisfies and sustains me in my good times, in between tough and challenging times. In Jesus's name, I pray. Amen.

The Twilight Hour

For ye were sometimes darkness, but now are ye light in the Lord: walk as children of the light.

—Ephesians 5:8 KJV

My journey began on the morning of July 11, 1994. For most people, it was just another ordinary day, but for me, it was survival. The beginning of my rebirth into a new life. I became renewed, refilled, and refreshed all because of God's grace and mercy toward me. After twenty-three years of torturing myself with drugs, alcohol, poor choices, seeking the approval of others about my life and who they thought I should be or not. The desire to be popular among the hip crowd and, most importantly, thinking I could do this on my own. At times I felt and hungered for a change within myself. The question was, how? Every time I tried to clean up my life, I would fall right back into a despaired, disillusioned lifestyle. Going back to my junior high school years, I learned from watching other rejects how to masquerade. The thing about masquerading is, I could lie to myself. I thought I could deceive those around me. I remember my parents who constantly reminded me as a kid, even into my adulthood/motherhood, "Victoria, you're not doing anything new that hasn't been done before." "The thing that hath been, it is that which shall be; and that which is done is that which shall be done: and there is no new thing under the sun" (Ecclesiastes 1:9 KJV).

By the time I turned thirty-seven, my life was out of control. I was drowning in crack, alcohol, beer, weed, prescription medication, along with losing hope that I could ever live a good and productive life. As long as I drank and got high, I felt it would assist me in running from myself and living the continual delusional lie that all might be well. In between my runs, which was daily, I would think about my children; how much I loved them and how I longed to be back in their lives; what I could've been, wanted to be, or should've been. I messed up; I fell victim to drugs and alcohol, falling to the point where this ugly, filthy habit controlled my life in such a way that I turned away from everything I loved, everything I desired to be. By the time 1994 rolled around, I began to hunger for my children, to be a part of the family again, to be that daughter, sister, friend, neighbor, mother, and a functional human being. What it would be like to be a productive mother again, to be there for them, to stop imagining what I could do and what I was supposed to do, to be a responsible mother, but how could I do that if every time I ended up getting high again!

It was February 1988; the birth of my last child was my first ever encounter with CPS (Child Protective Service). It was during then I met with Mrs. W, who approved for my youngest child to come home. About a month or so later, I received a telephone call from Mrs. K, the school's social worker at Sir Francis Drake. She informed me of the referral for me from DHS-CPS. I was required to meet with her, which I did. It was a group of several other mothers who had similar issues to mine. We would have group discussions about what was happening in our lives, but that didn't last too long. Mrs. K was in a car accident where she was injured and had to be hospitalized. She came back to school for several more sessions; I stopped going, and as far as I know, there was no replacement or referral to go somewhere else. Before the school year was over, from what I was told, she resigned due to health issues from the car accident. Unfortunately, I was weak, so instead of working on myself and taking care of my children, I chose to keep getting high. By the time December 1988 came around, I allowed the courts to turn my children, my responsibility, over to my mother.

From January 1, 1989, to July 9, 1994, my life was a living hell: sleeping on anyone's couch, eating out of soup kitchens, and lodging in homeless shelters. I got to know where to go to eat lunch and dinner. Providence Baptist Church on Wednesday for lunch. On Saturday mornings at St. John's MBC for prayer and breakfast. At St. John's, I would use the women's room to wash up and change my clothes. St. Anthony's and Glide in the Tenderloin, and St. Martin De Porres on Potrero Avenue. I even got arrested twice and served three months in SF County Jail on a bench warrant for a failure to appear.

By mid-1989, Bill and I got a nice studio in the Mission District at the King's Hotel. It was nice; we had our own bathroom, a small kitchenette. It was nice, but we ended up getting evicted, falling behind on the rent due to crack smoking. By mid-1993, I would try to quit crack. I would go the first three to five days smoking weed and drinking beer. I would even let my money stay on the books at the store where I cashed my checks. In fact, I even let my mother hold my money, but with her, that didn't last long. Nothing worked; I still kept running back to crack and hard liquor. I kept falling backward; I kept falling down. After losing my room at the Ambassador Hotel, I resorted to seeking shelter at the Sanctuary. Once I stayed at the shelter for thirty days. It was nice; I had a roommate. We would talk mostly about our lives, what we wanted out of life.

Every morning, rain or shine or in-between, we had to leave by 8:00 a.m. and come back by 5:00 p.m. for check-in, dinner at 6:00 p.m., along with 12-step meetings several nights a week. I was able to refrain from crack and hard liquor because I couldn't afford to lose my bed space. That itself proved I could kick my drug habit, but that green-eyed monster in me always showed up, and I'd end up using. All it took was check day (which was the first and fifteenth of each month), a can of beer, and a joint, then I was off to the crack races. I would also get with my boyfriend; he had a camper truck he lived in. It had hot and cold running water and a countertop stove. That was such a stormy time. I would stay with him in the camper truck in between our arguments and me getting ghost. (*Get ghost* means "disappearing, getting high somewhere else with other people.")

Finally, in the early 1990s, we decided to get a room with our GA income. The only place available was in the Tenderloin. From 1982 until 1985, my father lived at the Ambassador Residential Hotel at the corners of Mason and Eddy Streets in the Tenderloin before moving into the Rosa Parks Senior Apartments, where he resided until his passing on January 18, 1992. I asked my pop about the rooms; he told me they still rented rooms, but the hotel was accommodating HIV-AIDS patients. I talked it over with Bill; we put our money together and got us a room with our own bathroom at the Ambassador. The hotel has many amenities to accommodate the residents: this priest would come from Saint Boniface Catholic Church weekly for group sessions, the public health nurse would come, there were paid surveys for heterosexual couples as well as same-sex couples. The Sisters of Mercy would come to the hotel every single day to deliver lunch and dinners to those with HIV-AIDS. At times I would assist them, and for that, I would be rewarded with a meal. I tell you, those meals were good. Bill and I lived there for nearly two years. We had our own bathroom along with a mini refrigerator, a two-grill hot plate, and a mini-toaster oven. It wasn't so bad; we could've, I could've gotten somewhere, but my drug usage always stood in the way of my sanity, my desires to want to do right, and rational thinking.

After getting busted once in 1988 and 1989, I was given a court date for May 1, 1990, at 9:00 a.m., which was scheduled after my second drug arrest in August 1989. I was up early. I went to the check-cashing store at Seventh and Market Streets to pick up and cash my GA check. This is where the Department of Social Services sent the general-assistance checks for those like me in the Tenderloin/South of Market who didn't have an address. I signed for my check, got it cashed, then I started thinking. I thought, *Should I or shouldn't I go to court?* I decided not to appear. I boldly walked down Sixth Street behind the Hall of Justice on Harrison Street. I waited for the 9 San Bruno and headed out to Third Street.

Not realizing, or maybe I didn't care, that down the line, there would be a consequence called "bench warrant" for failing to appear. It was around January 1991, and it's check day, early evening. We were already high and had been drinking. My boyfriend and I got to fighting and arguing about something. I was yelling and screaming; it interfered with some of the other tenants getting high themselves. As a result, the police were called; my boyfriend was hauled off to jail. My consequence for failure to appear happened on that Friday morning. I was in bed asleep; there was a knock at the door. It was the police who came to arrest me. Their claim was, they were cleaning out their system and my name showed up having a bench warrant. I was like, "What's that?" The officer said, "You didn't keep your court date." I was convicted to two months in women's detention in San Francisco County Jail in San Bruno, California.

I don't know what I was thinking or why I felt like going to jail was some sort of badge of honor. What I did find out was, jail is a controlled environment that offers no real hope. It's a matter of survival. While I was down, I had one visitor, which was fine for me because I really didn't want my family to see me like this. I realized how embarrassing it was to get arrested, strip-searched, having to squat three times along with bending and coughing with each squat. One of my friends found out I was in the county jail, and she surprised me with a visit. She told me her nephew was in the men's jail, so she came to visit me. I don't know how she did it, but it was very refreshing and nice she did that. She was my only human contact with the outside world at that time, aside from the telephone calls and writing letters to my family, mainly my children. The letters usually consisted of "I'm okay, just counting the days to my release."

Once again, my father was not happy, especially since I was in jail, but he still looked out for me by taking care of my business, making sure my part of the rent was paid, then sent the rest to me by money order. The truth be told, I didn't trust my boyfriend, and they would not have let him sign my check. Since the hotel clerks knew my father, it was easy to make sure my portion of the rent got paid. The food stamps were split between my family, leaving me some food stamps and money on the books, which I rarely spent, by the way. While in lockup, I found a way to stay out of trouble and away from the troublemakers by reading books. I also attended various Christian church services and daytime activities. The Salvation Army facilitated arts, crafts, and letter writing. There were several wom-en's studies classes taught by several local colleges and universities. There were a couple of women I hung out with, along with minding my own business. But more importantly, keeping my money on the books.

Upon my release, I had a court appearance. The judge informed me I would be on probation for three years, then she looked at me with this nice nasty smile and informed me that if I get caught with any type of paraphernalia or drugs, I would be arrested and sent to state prison. Now that put the fear in me. The thought of going to prison, that was something I couldn't bear. Hearing stories of what goes down in women's prison, I would rather die than go to prison. For the first week or so, I followed the judge's orders: I made one visit to my probation officer, and that was it. As far as I could recall, she never called me or left messages at my mom's to see how I was doing. She never mandated me to come in for weekly or monthly visits, and she would've telephoned my mom's if she needed to leave a message or see how I was doing. I didn't have an ankle bracelet or was mandated to come in for UA (urine analysis) test for drugs and/ or alcohol in my system. I was on probation; I continued to smoke and use drugs, managing not to get caught and violating my proba-tion. Whew.

While living at the Ambassador, I started going to various pro-grams and support groups. At the time, they didn't work for me because I wasn't able to combat my drug and alcoholism. I enrolled for several certified courses at Southeast Community College, Business Machine Technology (BMT), which was learning to repair typewriters. I eventually dropped out after three weeks. Sometime later, I enrolled for a Home Health Aide thirty-day course. I had a chance to get my certificate. All I had to do was complete three days, but instead, I ended up using. What made this part of my life such a waste was the fact that the counselor, Mrs. Johnson, knew me from attending the Skill Center on top of the Hill during the mid-1980s, and now here I am, a dope fiend, a crackhead. For the record, after I got clean, I went back to Southeast to see her before her retirement.

As I struggled to get clean, I did it my way. I would smoke weed and drink beer from the first to the fifth and fifteenth to the twentieth of the month. I felt like I could minimize. I would go to Glide every first and fifteenth, from noon to 6:00 p.m., movie day. This was to deter drug usage by airing four or six movies with all-you-can-eat hot dogs, soda, juice, and popcorn. "For free." It was a place to come alone, bring a friend or family. I would also go to see the counselors; I needed someone to talk to, vent, someone to listen to me. I even signed up for day treatment at Glide. After three weeks and money in my pocket, all it took was that one hit, and I was right back on the crack run again. What I didn't realize was, I had to abstain from all drugs and alcohol, including beer and weed. In the meantime, I continued living homeless in shelters and on people's couches. I was surviving, hustling cans and bottles, messing around with a few old drunks for a couple of dollars, and visiting my children in between. Every now and then, I would still go to Mass.

My last visit to Mass during my addiction was when I got the idea to steal some of the collection money. I had gone to the altar to pray, and I noticed that when Mass was over, the collection basket was left at the foot of the altar. So the plan was, the following Sunday, I was going to go to the altar and pray. I couldn't wait for the following Sunday; I had it all planned. I would go to the altar, then indiscreetly dip my hand in the basket and steal some of the collection money. Sunday had arrived. I was all pious; I was clean, and I even had a good night's sleep. I went to Mass, saw my family; after Mass, they left. So I made my move to the altar. I'm literally ready to steal from God; how low-down could I get? I went to the altar and, to my surprise, the collection plate was gone. My first thought was, what dirty lowlife took the basket? You're talking about mad. After I got clean and shared this story in my support group and 12-step group, we laughed about this, but the reality was, I was so sick that I was willing to steal from the church. God really had my back; he really and truly did.

I continued to go to Glide to see the counselors; I'd go for meals or whatever they had to offer. I was thinking about being a mother, asking myself what happened to me. I wanted to stop; I would think about earlier times when I would go grocery shopping, cook for my babies. I really began to see this was not the life I wanted. I had dreams; I had goals. What happened to me? How did I get into this mess? I needed help; what was I going to do? Then it happened; it was early in the morning, June 1994, on my friend's back porch. I could see the Twin Peaks. It was around 4:00 a.m., and I started praying to God, but it went from a prayer to a conversation. I didn't realize it then; it was the beginning of a life I never thought I would ever have. Instead of praying for finding money or hoping that Bill and I could get married, I asked God, what was wrong with me? I tried everything I could think of to stay off drugs. I would even minimize my drug/alcohol usage from the first to the fourth and fifteenth to the nineteenth; I would smoke weed and drink beer. Or I would leave money at the store so I wouldn't spend it all in a day and a half. I tried to change my life, but nothing worked; having extra money would only lead me back to crack, hard liquor, and stealing. "For that which I do I allow not" (Romans 7:15); "For the earnest expectation of the creature waiteth for the manifestation of the sons of God" (Romans 8:19).

As I was praying/talking to God, a miracle happened. All of a sudden, the sky opened up; it was around 4:00 a.m., there was a bright light that stretched across Twin Peaks. This was the final week of my getting high and drinking; as the weekend approached, it was different. Saturday, July 9, 1994, was an unusual day; I didn't get high. It was sunny out, but the atmosphere was weird. Around 3:00 p.m., I was in the parking lot of Super Save. There was this one woman whose house I would go to, but when she got high, her tweak was "not to shut up"; she talked, she talked, and she talked. Of course, if I came across drugs, I was welcomed to her house. That day she asked me to come to her house. As night fell, I ran into this guy James I knew. He worked in construction, and when he got paid, he would get so drunk he was easy to clip. Several weeks earlier, he stated he was going to pretend he was drunk, then whoever was clipping him, he was going to break the person's arm. I was going to call his bluff, but what happened was, I was so tired and sleepy from being high I fell asleep in his car. Around 1:30 a.m., we both awoke;

I told him I was going up to Cashmere. He said his clutch was bad, so he couldn't drive me up to Cashmere and LaSalle. I told him that it was okay; I walked to my friend's apartment. Although it was 2:00 a.m., he let me in. I was so tired I fell asleep on the couch. When morning came, he told me to come back for dinner; he was cooking red beans with pork rinds, over rice and corn bread. This old man could throw down. I told him I would be back around 4:00 p.m., but I never went back.

I don't really recall much of that day, except I collected cans and bottles, cashed them in at JR's; he worked at a recycling/metal yard. After hours and weekends, he bought cans, redemption glass, and plastic at half the price the metal yard paid. Afterward, around four o'clock, I stopped at Ora Lee's house. She lived on Kirkwood Avenue, the next block over from Momma. I went to tell her I was going to get myself together and I wanted to say goodbye. She asked where I was going; I told her I was going to the shelter and I wanted to get there in time for 6:00 p.m. dinner call. She said she was moving to Sacramento; she said, "You're going to need some cigarettes." She gave me $5.00 for cigarettes (at that time, Dorel cigarettes were three packs for $4.50). As I came out of the store, I ran into Bill; he was talking to some chick we both knew, and they looked at me, and I looked at them. I took Ora Lee's change back to her. We hugged each other, and that was the last time I saw her. I headed on across town to the shelter on Polk and Geary to get a bed and make it on time for the 6:00 p.m. dinner call.

The first three days after leaving the shelter, each morning I would catch the bus to Momma's to get my grocery cart filled with the aluminum cans, plastic, and glass bottles I stacked up the day before, go to the recycling and metal yard to cash them in, then head to Glide for group. But that Wednesday, July 13, 1994, was the day I was going to live or die. After I dropped off my bottles and plastic on Donner Street, I was headed toward the metal yard on Evans Street to turn in my cans. When I got to Mendell Street and Newcomb Avenue in front of the opera house, something triggered inside me: "good versus evil." A guy I went to elementary school with, who was a crack dealer, had his Caddy parked in front of the opera house. It was the ten o'clock hour, and that alter ego voice in my head said, "It's okay, no one will know." The right side of my head said, "Don't do it." That wicked spirit wanted to take control, but that righteous voice overpowered that evil side. The righteous prevailed and said to me, "You run like hell, and don't you ever look back." I pushed that cart with the garbage bag full of aluminum cans down Mendell Street, made a left on Jerrold Avenue, crossed Third Street, and went in the back way on the train tracks to the metal yard. I parked that cart, turned in my cans, and collected my money. I headed to the 19 Polk bus stop on Evans Street across from the metal yard, went to Glide, and never looked back. You have to understand why I praise God so much. It was a beautiful summer morning, Wednesday, July 13, 1994, that could've turned into complete darkness, but because I kept my word with God, he made it shine for me. Hallelujah.

This picture was taken around March 1994, after I got out of jail. As you can see, I was in bad shape. I only took this because I needed my California ID for check cashing, medical and social services business, and other identification purposes. When I first got clean, I didn't care about my outward appearance; it was my soul, it was my life I was fighting for. For once, I was able to get my foot in the door and stay there. "For I will restore health unto thee" (Jeremiah 30:17 KJV).

Where Do I Sign?

> For everyone that asketh receiveth; and he
> that seeketh findeth; and to him that knocketh it
> shall be opened.

> —Matthew 7:8 KJV

It was a tug-of-war morning of why or why I should not cop some dope. You could say it was more than what I bargained for. After dropping off my cans, I hopped on the 19 Polk. I finally arrived at Glide; my counselor says they're starting a new generation. It was a twenty-week outpatient treatment program. I jumped at the opportunity. I said, "Yes." She gave me the paperwork; I signed up quickly, fast, and in a definite hurry. This is the opportunity I've been waiting for; now I can get myself together and stop getting high. The counselors are supportive and friendly. This is definitely the place I belong. I soon learned it would take more than just quitting drugs and alcohol for my life to get back on track. I found out that I would have to "process my feelings" and "be honest." In other words, I had to "tell my business," which meant no more lying, fabricating stories, telling everything that's going on with me, and most of all, no more victimizing myself, which was the best part of my distorted life because I didn't have to take responsibility for my ill-gotten actions and behavior. It sucked because, as long as I was the victim, I could blame others for the problems that I created or at least was a part of. In order to recover or heal, I had to face the unbearable "truth." It was decades of bad habits, suffering from depression, and other problems I had that contributed to my using drugs and alcohol: spending twenty-three years of living outside myself, seeking the need to be liked by others, giving up my children, lying, sexual trauma, rage, stealing, and the psychological damage by others and myself. "There hath no temptation taken you but such as is common to man, but God is faithful, who will not suffer you to be tempted above that ye are able" (1 Corinthians 10:13), "Be sober, be vigilant; for your adversary the devil, as a roaring lion, walketh about, seeking whom he may devour" (1 Peter 5:8 KJV), "For all that is in the world, the lust of the flesh, the lust of the eyes, and the pride of life, is not of the Father, but is of the world" (1 John 2:16 KJV).

This was going to require a lot of work, way more than I anticipated. "Working on my insides." Really? Seriously? I was so desperate and determined to clean up my life. I was willing and ready to do whatever I needed to get off drugs once and for all. Period. After all, I made a promise to God that if he helped me out, I would clean up my life, never to use again. If working on my insides or whatever was needed to be done to get myself together, then so be it. At this point in my life, I had nothing to lose. Eventually, maybe several years down the line, I came to realize it wasn't going to be my way but the way that God ordained. For once in my life, I had to shut the heck up, stop crying, stop lying, stop manipulating, be humble, and listen. I had to face the truth about the real me, and it wasn't pretty, and it certainly wasn't pleasant, but it saved my life. "Heal me, O Lord, and I shall be healed; save me, and I shall be saved: for thou art my praise" (Jeremiah 17:14 KJV).

Enrolling in this program saved my life. It was, and still is, a daily program for me. The good news is being able to work at one's own pace. When one is serious about a goal or a determination, the light goes on, but nothing gets done in a day, a week, or even a month. There were times when sobriety was one hour at a time. Part of the day treatment was attending several outside meetings; each client was given attendance sheets for the meeting secretaries or facilitators to sign. I made at least seven 12-step meetings a week. I had to learn to shut up, pay attention, wait my turn, raise my hand when I wanted to share, and if I didn't get called on, then learn not to make a big deal of it. I would journal or maybe talk with someone after the meeting. This was important for me because I loved to talk. I realized talking was one of my biggest issues, and at times I talked too much, told business that needed to be reserved for prayer or someone I knew would understand. This led me to journaling. I love reading, so I made it my business to read the 12-step literature and the books, reading the twelve steps and traditions over and over again. For me, even to this day, the twelve steps were and are kind of like the Ten Commandments. They were important, lifesaving rules to follow in order for me to stay clean. Just like the Ten Commandments, they're not options. I didn't understand the testimonials at first, but the more my head got unclouded and even attending the meetings, I began to see the connections between me and the writer.

Recovery meant facing the fact that I had bad habits, issues, and problems that needed to be addressed if there was any chance of me living a life without drugs or alcohol. That meant showing up every day at the program, even if I got jacked up, was confronted about my issues, or had my counselor put something on the floor that I said or did. One thing I discovered or faced after I got clean was that sex was not something I always consented to; it was needed in order for me to survive in the wretched world I lived in. There were at times situations such as an exchange for one night's room and board. Recovery meant that I had to face the fact that I used drugs and alcohol because it was so much better for me to cover up the lies, keep telling myself, convincing myself, and justifying that it was okay to get high. When I did wrong to others, then have the "I don't care" attitude, I'll just get high; that way, I don't have to deal with reality. Recovery meant I had to learn to make my own decisions without being under the influence of drugs and alcohol. I had the right to make my own decisions, not allow others to dictate to me what they think I should be, do, say, or think. I'm not only making wise decisions at thirty-seven and a half years old, but I would also have to act on them, develop plans, follow them through, and be accountable to myself in front of the group or one-on-one with my therapist or counselor. "God, why is this so difficult? Can I just stay clean and skip the informal formalities?"

At a time when running away by using drugs and drinking would be my decision, changing myself became a part of my life I can truly say I wasn't ready for what or what was to come. As this change came about, sitting in "the circle" Monday through Friday for twenty weeks, dealing with rules, regulations, circle time, support groups, me getting put on front street, "I was being exposed," "I couldn't blame others for my problems anymore," "I mean, I didn't mind telling others what they needed to do, but I certainly didn't like it when I was confronted." Another challenge in the first few months in the program, it never failed; every first and fifteenth (if they fell on weekdays), I was confronted in the group, yeah, in front of everyone: Was I going to go see my boyfriend? Was I going to give him my money? Am I going to get high? Questions, questions, questions—it drove me crazy, but I was determined to keep my promise with God. He helps me, and I stay clean.

As for me and my newfound life, I was attending 12-step meetings, living in the shelter's recovery section, and getting to Glide every single day. They were places of safe refuge for me. Reporting to someone else gave me the strength needed to survive. Most of all, I had to be accountable. There was mandatory drug testing, I believe, on Thursdays. The following Tuesday, dirty results were read aloud in class; therefore, it was definitely much easier for me to just stay clean. I couldn't bear being busted out like that. Knowing me, if I had relapsed, I wouldn't have gone back to the program anyway. At the end of the day, I would much rather get jacked up by my counselors than go back out and use.

What gave me hope in my early beginnings in recovery was that no one snickered behind my back when I spoke about how I felt. There was no two-facedness around me. When I was in need of food, clothing, or a place to rest, I didn't have to compromise myself, or when talking to guys, there were no sexual negotiations. I could have a decent conversation with men and be okay with that. Most of all, going to classes that dealt with the seven wheels of abuse, domestic violence, love/relationships, and other groups. There were evening therapeutic groups from 6:00 p.m. to 8:00 p.m. that covered my daytime classes, which made it more open and intimate for me to go into depth, especially since several of these support groups were "women only" with a female therapist/facilitator. I have to thank God for my two friends who worked at the shelter, because before I got clean, they always made sure when I checked in, I had a bed. Once I got clean, it was one of them who told me to speak with the shelter case manager about a bed in the recovery section, which was great because I no longer had to check in daily; I was assigned a bed.

This story I have to tell because it was one of many that changed my life. One meeting in particular I would attend was in the Marina District, not far from Galileo, my high school alma mater. It was a weekday midmorning AA meeting where I was the only woman. Due to my drug/alcohol addiction, I had developed a perception of men. You know, give and take. You help me out, give me a place to crash, they get drunk, I get high, so when the subject of sex came up, no matter how repulsive I thought it was, it was the price I paid for their "generosity." But due to God's grace and mercy putting me in that particular place, that particular meeting, I could learn and understand that the average man was and is not a womanizer, the average man is not an abuser, and most of all, the average man does care for and respect the female species. I can hug men and they can hug me without some sordid expectation. I learned a lot from these men. I learned about friendship, that it's okay for men and women to simply be friends. In fact, the woman who worked at this meeting facility looked at me as I was leaving a meeting one day and said to me, "Here, I have something for you, read this." At first, I glanced at the title, thinking it was a steamy novel. It turned out to be a book written by a female psychologist on women and codependency. This book, along with me attending a weekly codependency group, really helped out a lot. I felt obligated to jump in voluntarily to help people, then when I needed help, I would get upset because they didn't read my mind or just jump right in and reciprocate. I also learned that codependency can begin in childhood.

The work was continual and at times overwhelming. My comfort zone of places was challenged. I was so connected and used to living and hanging out in the Tenderloin, a.k.a. TL, Hunter's Point, Fillmore, or East Oakland. I wasn't stupid or anything like that; I was well aware of other places I dreamed of. I just didn't see myself going to those places. The comfort zone that I could only be friends with Black people proved false. I had, and still have, friends of different nationalities. Just to go back to my high school days, at Galileo, which was majority Chinese and other nationalities, opened the door, but I really didn't understand. God introduced me to his great big world that I can be a part of. I can make a contribution, and eventually, down the line, I would be able to help others make a difference in their lives as well. I found out from working with Hispanics, Asians, Black Africans, Caribbeans, and other nationalities that we have shared similarities: faith, family, hospitality, history, and hard work.

In the program, everything was happening fast, but it was like an order. I had issues that needed to be addressed. Unfortunately, my father didn't live to see me get clean. This weighed on me; it was a pressing feeling of guilt and hurt that I couldn't say I'm sorry or I couldn't hear him say, "I knew you could do it." Pops passed away in his sleep on January 18, 1992, and here it was two years later, me sitting in the afternoon group in Freedom Hall, and it hit me. I remember feeling blue, and I started talking about him. I was apprehensive, but I had to get this weight off my chest. I cried because I actually told what happened. On that Wednesday, January 15, he asked me to stay overnight. I owed him fifteen dollars; I didn't have it, and he said it was alright. The following night, he was gone. I managed to get into the building, I made my way into his apartment, he wasn't at home, and I stole a few dollars from him. Not understanding, with my mind on getting high, I just didn't understand. The next thing I knew, I got the phone call he was gone. The group facilitator said to me, "It's okay, you need to let it go." She also said to me I never had the time to grieve or even process. No one laughed at me or told me to get out. I was also able to talk about it one-on-one with my therapist. I was thinking my father didn't live to see me get clean, like Moses didn't live to see the people make it to the Promised Land (Joshua 1:1–11 KJV).

No matter what, I showed up every single day to the program. Then several of my counselors would tell me I wasn't going to make it. One day, during the eleven o'clock group, one of the male counselors fronted me off in front of everyone. He said to me, "You know you want to get high." He literally reached into his pocket and threw twenty dollars in the middle of the circle. Now my pride was at stake; I'm thinking, *You're fronting me off in front of everyone.* I thought, *What if I just snatch that money up off the floor and put it in my pocket?* I wanted to show him up, you know, make a fool out of him. The other counselors and the other clients watched. I swallowed my pride, left the twenty dollars on the floor, and stayed clean. Another time, about the sixth week into the program, I was still carrying two bags of papers and drinking my soda in a bag, like a can of beer. There I was, minding my own business, and bam, it happened. It was "pick on Vickie" day in the eleven o'clock group. One of my male counselors said to me, "Is that a beer in the bag?" I said in a sarcastic tone, "No." Then one thing led to another, and I ended up having to write five pages on carrying an open can of soda in a paper bag like it was a can of beer. It was due that Wednesday. Oh, and here's the kicker: I gave him the written assignment; he looked at it and tossed it in the garbage.

I was one month into my recovery / the program when I had the seizure during "circle time." I didn't feel it coming on, and by the time I regained consciousness, one of my counselors and eighteenth-generation member picked me up from SF General Hospital and took me back to the shelter. Upon the discharge that afternoon, I was given a follow-up appointment. Then that doctor scheduled me to see a neurologist. I kept my appointment, which I'm glad I did, because the brain scan also played a role in how I lived my life from that moment on. The "verdict" was that my brain was that of a sixty-four-year-old person, and I was only thirty-eight years old. This was due to several decades of drug and alcohol usage. There was no treatment, medication, or surgery that would help. There was one remedy and one remedy only: it was to stay clean. The neurologist was very compassionate to me as I sat there, looking at the brain scan pictures. He even asked me if I needed a moment to myself. I told him I was okay, and then he explained that the seizure was triggered because I had not been using, which was confusing because my seizures were usually triggered due to my daily, consistent drug and alcohol usage.

I found out that in the State of California, when a person has a sei-zure or a brain/head injury, the Department of Motor Vehicles is notified, and if the person is a licensed driver, then that person's driv-er's license is placed on hold for a year. For me, living in the TL, there was plenty of public transportation accessibility; this qualified me for a disabled bus pass, which I was able to use to pay discount prices on all the Bay Area systems: Cal-Train, BART, AC Transit—you name it. Due to good, steady, no-cost health care, along with having a pri-mary doctor, I was able to take care of myself and ask questions. My primary told me anything I needed, to talk to him first and he would direct me to whatever medical services I needed.

About seven weeks into the program, I arrived early, so I stopped in the office. One of my female counselors asked me about my two bags and what was in them. I told her it was my personal belongings and important papers. Before I got clean, my whole life was in two plastic grocery bags. I had papers and a few personal items like soap, deodorant, a washcloth, and undergarments. She looked at me and said in amazement, "Victoria, I don't believe it, you're a real live bag lady." Even though I smiled, I was embarrassed when she said that to me; in all honesty, it was embarrassing living the homeless life, living a life that I created due to my drug habit.

My assignment from her was to go through my bags and deter-mine what was worth keeping, then meet with her to discuss the bag issue, its contents, and why I was packing this stuff around. Most of the papers were ambulance bills from seizures I had during the last five years of my addiction. With the help of my counselor and the program's executive director, I was able to schedule a court date at city hall to deal with these delinquent medical bills. I went to court and explained to the judge that I had no money to pay off these debts, along with a letter verifying I was in the program and a notice of action that I was receiving general assistance. The judge reviewed the ambulance bills and threw them all out, every single bill. I was no longer in that debt, which felt good. From that moment on, I was never the "bag lady" anymore.

As I stated earlier in this chapter, my two friends told me about recovery beds, so I met with the case manager because the shelter had recovery beds for men and women in drug treatment programs. I told my counselor, then met with the shelter's case manager. I got the forms signed, and the following day, I no longer had to sign up nightly for a bed. The basic house rules still applied: breakfast for women at 6:00 a.m., sign out by 8:00 a.m., and I usually signed in by 5:30, which gave me time to get settled and prepared for dinner, which for the women was at 6:00 p.m. I stayed busy, made a few friends, watched television, and talked. I made it a point to be respectful toward everyone. I followed the house rules, and most of all, this was a good way to work my program. On Wednesday evening from 8:00 to 9:00 p.m., there was an AA meeting, and on Thursday nights, the big meeting: from 8:00 to 10:00 p.m. were NA meetings. This was an open meeting for outsiders to attend as well. I got to know the men and women at the shelter who were in recovery. I still see and communicate with many friends I met in recovery; some, like me, have committed themselves to Jesus Christ. What a blessing to know the Ten Commandments and the 12 steps. What I love and got out of this process is becoming a "new creature in Christ Jesus." Being clean and sober while living in a controlled and safe environment also came with challenges that were totally unexpected. There were two incidents; I forgot which occurred first: It was early one morning, before I got my recovery bed, around 3:00 a.m. I was suddenly awakened by a commotion, and lights were on. One of the women died that morning. One of the floor counselors attempted to resuscitate her, but she was gone. I looked out the window at Post and Polk; at that time, there was a liquor store. Honest to goodness, that store was open, and my first thought was to go get a drink. When I looked again, the store was closed. Since this happened in the middle of the week, I processed it in "the circle," one-on-one with my counselor, and shared at a meeting later that day. The second one was Columbus Day weekend. I was at Bill's, so here it was that Sunday; it was nice out. I was washing clothes; I took the last load out of the dryer. Bill lived in a duplex; the owner, who was his friend and employer, bought a washer and dryer for both tenants. I dumped the load onto the bed to fold and put away; all of a sudden, there was this little plastic bag with a ten-dollar piece of crack. See, the couple on the ground floor were smokers; the wife would hide crack from her husband. Honest to goodness, that little piece of crack in that baggie reached up and grabbed me by my collar and pulled me down. There I was, face-to-face. I got down on my knees, then I raised my head, peering at that plastic baggie and the contents in it. You should've seen me crawling on my knees and peering at that baggie. I realized the sun was out, the game was almost over, and Bill was headed to West Oakland. My head started talking to me, "You can smoke this piece of crack, no one will ever know." The stumbling block was, once I smoked this piece of crack, the monster in me would've come back to life. Since I had money, I'd need more crack, cigarettes, weed, and liquor. Then Tuesday, I'd have to go back to the program, or if I went back, then I would've had to face the counselors, the executive director, and my classmates, and they would be able to tell. After they would've torn me up, knowing them, they would've UA-ed me that very moment (UA is for *urinalysis*), instead of waiting for Wednesday, the regular weekly UA day. I already knew this wasn't going to work, so I called Bill into the room, showed him what I found, and gave it to him. He said, "I know what to do with it." For the record, he didn't smoke it. After Bill left to go to West Oakland, I called this woman I met at a meeting and told her what happened. I went to a meeting later that evening the next day to share about what happened. On Tuesday, I shared in the circle, met with my counselor one-on-one and at another meeting. Even though I faced these two challenges in my early recovery, I made it. I survived. I didn't get high. You know, it reminds me of two scriptures: "If any man becomes new in Christ, old things pass away" (2 Corinthians 5:17 KJV). "Submit yourselves therefore to God. Resist the devil, and he will flee from you" (James 4:7 KJV).

After twenty weeks, it's Sunday morning, December 4, 1994, at Glide's 11:00 a.m. service, and the nineteenth generation graduation. The program's executive director, all our counselors, our friends from the previous generations, and of course, the congregation were there to support us. Along with our certificates, we were given Bibles, which I would read and take to church with me. I believe I still have that Bible, along with the certificates I received from Glide. Later that day, I caught up with Bill, and we went to his aunt's house in Daly City, where we ended up spending the night. When I woke up the next morning, I knew then I was going to make it. For the first time in my life, I did something right. I did what I wanted to do, and I completed it, and it felt good; it felt real doggone good. The only bittersweetness was my father didn't live to see me get my life together, and that made me sad, but I could hear his encouraging words: "Victoria, I knew you could do it. I knew you could." He would've been right there, cheering me on with his great big smile, giving me a hug. Just thinking about how he would've felt made me happy again, along with my friends, Bill, and his aunt.

After the graduation from the program in December 1994, in January, I signed up for six more months in Glide's aftercare. I was still in the shelter's recovery section. Although my boyfriend had his own spot in North Oakland, it was time for me to live independently. The program director is working with me. I filled out applications at the Hamlin and Chamberlain clean and sober hotels in the TL. I was also running on my own will; the Sunday of the graduation, before meeting up with Bill, I was introduced to this woman by this brother in the rooms. She was presented as a landlord. She lived in the Glen Park district, not far from the Glen Park BART station. I went to her house, and it turns out she rents rooms, but for me, it was going to be the couch at $400 per month; she had lost her mind. What did it for me was, on the living room coffee table, there was a Ouija board. As far as I was concerned, this woman was on the dark side, and I wasn't having it. Plus, I would've been the only Black person in that house, and again, I wasn't having it. Despite the person I was, I knew God. I was raised up with him in my life, and even in the streets and in jail, I never stopped praying. I'd go to church every once in a while, getting the Word and singing hymns weekly at Providence and St. John's Baptist Church every Wednesday and Saturday.

Right before Christmas, I met with my shelter case manager. This woman informs me that January would be my last month at the shelter for several reasons: she presents me with a credit report she pulled without my knowledge. She showed me this report, and it had several names that were not mine; also there were several social security numbers. What puzzled me was why she would pull my credit report without my knowledge or consent. Why would she need to pull my credit report to stay for three more months at the shelter? She had no rational reason. The other lame reason was that I would leave on weekends and return Monday afternoon. Her claim was that I had only so many weekends to do that, and I exceeded the so-called limit. In the years of my addiction, drug/alcohol-induced seizures, or even getting arrested twice, I never used an alias: I always used my real name, social security, and personal information. I had enough problems in my life, and taking on an alias would only create more than I could handle. I think what it was, I saw her several months earlier at a Friday night AA meeting, which I thought was great. I mean, my counselors and the executive director at Glide were recovering addicts. Two of them served time in prison, and one served time in county jail. It was no big deal. God, being such an awesome God, while I was trying to figure out what I was going to do, already had a plan spinning.

My kindergarten picture in 1961 at Burnett
Elementary School, now Leona Havard.

This picture was taken in early 1973. I was attending
John Robert Powers modeling school in downtown
San Francisco. I was sixteen and a half.

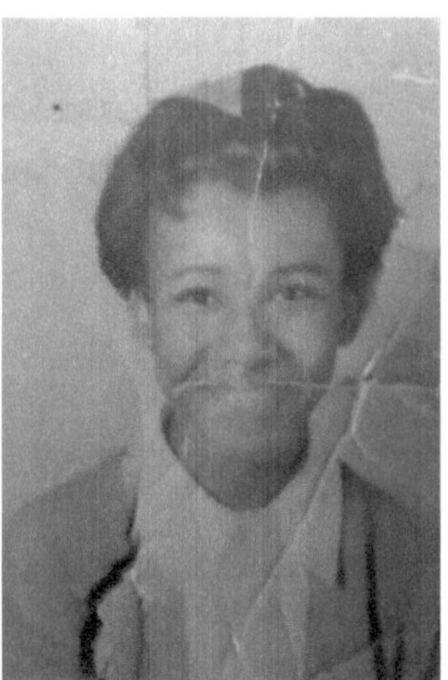

My sixth-grade picture at All Hallows 1968.

On my own

> Yea, though I walk through the valley of the
> shadow of death, I will fear no evil: for thou art
> with me; thy rod and thy staff they comfort me.
> (Psalm 23:4 KJV)

In January 1995, I was facing the possibility of getting evicted from the shelter. I was six months clean and sober, which in itself was amazing. I had a hearing centered on me leaving every weekend; the claim was I had used up my time. I told her, according to the shelter rules, I could stay away for up to seventy-two hours without losing my assigned bed. Then there was the bogus credit report; that really threw me, because why would she pull my credit report without my consent then confront me about alias names and several social security numbers that weren't mine? She made it clear I wasn't going to win this case, not because I did wrong, but as far as she was concerned, I had to go. Yes, I was worried because I hadn't found a place to live. In fact, I got turned down for both the Hamlin and Cambridge clean and sober hotels, and I knew I hadn't done anything wrong. But I had to fight this case for another three months at the shelter. I kept reading the Bible scripture "Do not worry" (Luke 12:22–31 KJV). I prayed, trusted in God, kept going to my meetings, and stayed clean. What I didn't realize was, God had already worked it out for me.

Fighting this battle with the shelter was my first major encounter advocating, navigating, and standing up for myself. On the flip side, there were two things occurring in my favor: the director and I walked up to the Arlington clean and sober hotel to meet with the manager. As we were talking, the manager said, "You're approved." I was so used to getting turned down or denied for a place I didn't hear what she said. The director looked at me with an excited smile and said, "You got approved." Then I reacted with a surprised smile. Whew, what a relief.

The next good thing was, I was selected to be interviewed by Channel 2 reporter Don K; this would happen on my last day at the shelter. The good news was, the hearing was canceled by me; the case manager never met with me to close out my case or even congratulate me, which I really didn't care about. As I left the shelter for the final time with the reporter standing there and the camera rolling, I was a celebrity that morning. I thank the line staff because they were the ones who made sure I got a bed, especially the swing shift staff. I also told the staff I would be back, not as a client, but as a visitor. I did come back, attending the Thursday night 12-step meeting from 8:00 to 10:00 p.m. As the reporter and I walked down to my new spot at the Arlington Hotel, we went up to my room to complete the interview. I believe I still have the VHS cassette tape. One of the questions was, how much would it take for me to live? I quoted at that time $1,000 a month. Now mind you, this was early 1995, so the cost of living was different from today, 2023. My rent alone was $325, along with other monthly obligations: my telephone bill, transportation, nonfood items, cable bill, and a little mad money.

In these first couple of years, life was routine; you can say it went well. "Lights, camera, action, gone." Here I am in my own place; the last time I had a place in my name was the Pink Palace, a.k.a. Yerba Buena Annex, from 1976 to 1980. I had a room, but I had to share a bathroom as well as the kitchen. When I first moved in, I got help from my Glide Facts on Crack family. The executive director bought me linen, and one of the other counselors talked with the head maintenance man at Glide; he repaired a thirteen-inch Sony color TV for me. One of my friends, a graduate of the eighteenth generation and like my recovery big sister, was moving out of the Arlington. She gave me her fridge with a lock on it and an oak desk, which was what I needed. In July 1995, I reenrolled at City College of San Francisco under the Second Chance program. The way I ended back in college was, two of my counselors were on the Second Chance panel at CCSF as well as alumni. This program targeted men and women who had been incarcerated, giving us the chance to return to college, obtain a degree or certificate, and from there, obtain gainful employment. This program was under the EOPS umbrella, provided vouchers for course books, materials, fee waiver, and if I'm correct, Muni bus passes. I also applied for financial aid, but because in the 1980s I attended CCSF and withdrew, I was on financial aid probation. I couldn't get financial aid in the fall of 1995, but I got financial assistance from the Second Chance Program. Being on GA and food stamps was not enough for me to live off. Bill and I had a friend who was a Muni driver at the time. I told him I was looking for a job. He told me his wife was a supervisor at a home health care agency on Tenth and Mission Streets in San Francisco. He gave me her number; I called her, and she told me to come on down. I completed the paperwork, and I was hired. It worked out fine because I worked three days per week and attended school twice a week.

I completed my fall courses with good grades. In the spring of 1996, I petitioned to get off financial aid probation, and it was granted. I was able to get my financial aid monies and work-study. I got a little over nine hundred dollars, so I covered any other school necessities, and I went to the dentist and got me a nice set of dentures. Oh, I forgot to mention the dope, alcohol, cigarettes, weed, poor eating habits, and lack of dental care is how I lost my teeth. This was one of the biggest regrets in my life.

What I've learned then and understand now is that after twenty-seven years of sobriety, recovery was, is, and always will be a lifetime process for me. There were so many dreams and goals for me to achieve. But at that time in 1994, there were so many issues I had to work on. My life and sanity were at stake. The biggest one was relationships: developing a relationship with myself and where I was standing with Bill. At the time I decided to get clean, we had been together for sixteen years. Before, I was incapable of making this radical, life-changing decision.

I had to start dealing with my relationship between me and Bill because it was shifting. Even though I had my own place to live, I would still go to Oakland and hang out with him. I still loved him, I wanted to be with him, and I wanted me, him, and the kids to be a family again. I was clean and sober, attending meetings, yet I was still cursing him out and calling him names. I wanted to hurt him, make him feel bad, feel sorry for the fact that we didn't get married, we weren't the family I would imagine us to be. I was addicted, lost the kids, and became homeless; somebody had to be accountable. It was one Friday night, late spring or early summer 1995, we got to arguing. We were sitting in his truck. I cursed that man so bad. He didn't say anything or react, but when I looked at him, he was so sad that I said the things I said to him, and at that very moment, I knew then I needed some help. I had an anger problem, and I needed help. When that following Monday came, I was in the aftercare program; it just so happened a three-month Anger Management Group was starting. I signed up with the quickness. I also started getting more honest with my therapist, beefing up my 12-step meetings. This recovery was more than what I bargained for, but in order to stay clean, it didn't matter how other people, especially those in my life, wanted to live; I had to change. It was better to sit in a group and endure a few minutes of criticism than a lifetime of dysfunction.

I went to meetings and therapy groups to process, but going back to church, praying, and taking it to God became my guide on how and where to move to help myself. I learned that God moves, answers, and reveals in his time answers and solutions. One thing I'm constantly learning and having at times to stop and not to worry because my God reminds me in Matthew 6:25–34 KJV. Instead of drinking and drugging, live a natural lifestyle, take up exercise, jog, lift weights, or write a journal. Making sure to get a church home, mosque, or temple. Getting involved in a sisterhood, men's, young adults', teens', and children's group. These groups are spiritual and a great support system. Every year I'm including something new and exciting into my life: exercise, running in place, writing gospel songs, poems, being more financially minded, and journal writing. Take it from me: for God's sake, stay away from drugs, alcohol, weed, beer; that stuff is poison. It'll only warp your mind, damage your body, and steal your soul.

Micheal Stith aka Mike or in the family Mikey, my first born and only son. He served in the United States Navy, he's now a "Proud Veteran". Woot Woot

Taken April 2013 in momma's backyard before her passing
From left to right: Alexandra, Victoria (me), Maria and Juliana

Unexpected Reality Sets In

> But ye are a chosen generation, a royal priesthood, an holy nation, a peculiar people; that ye should shew forth the praises of him who hath called you out of darkness into his marvellous light.

> —1 Peter 2 KJV

The third year in recovery was a year of unexpected events beyond my control. Never mind relapsing; it was my sanity that was at stake. At first, getting clean meant to stop using. Again, I didn't expect or even realize that a part of getting clean is more than stopping the use of drugs and alcohol; it meant dealing with reality, all the time, anytime, anywhere. The reality is, I learned as a Christian and in recovery that because I'm clean, I will face temptation, family, job, social issues, life's problems, and good times. It's how I choose to deal with them and, most of all, turn to God for answers, wisdom, protection, and what to do about what I'm going through. *Note*: Notice I added "good times" because, when things are going well, that's when temptation and those old ways creep into my head, telling me it's okay to celebrate, it's okay to have a drink or beer, no one will know. Maybe at that moment no one will know, but God will know. And I can't live with using, drinking, and lying because, eventually, it will all come out. Even in good times, I choose prayer and enjoy those moments of good times.

Going back to my second year of sobriety, I was visiting my children as regularly and often as I could. What I really wanted was to get reunified with my children, but at the time, I was settling for overnight visits. Going to family court was useless because, at that time, the man over the bench was a commissioner and, from my observation, he didn't know what he was doing. Starting from the moment I met my court-appointed attorney in 1988, he has never shown or displayed any care, sympathy, or the desire to help me. He couldn't care less if I got my children back or not; he didn't care about me getting clean. I was just another caseload. With this so-called attorney of mine, it was always a continuance, and he always had less than two sentences to say if he said anything at all. I was tired of beating my head against the wall. I felt like a goldfish in a tank full of sharks gnawing away at me. Standing in front of this commissioner at a family court was pathetic. All he did was display his stupid grin, as the lawyers for both parties would shout "continuance." Once I got clean and sober, I saw my attorney for who he really was. It wasn't just me; it was other parents, especially other Black noncustodial parents. We would observe the behavior and lack of interaction between attorney and client. I knew something could be done; I just had to find the right resource, someone who would not only waste my time by letting me state my case then only to find out there's nothing I could do. But someone who would actually understand and care about me. I messed up, I made a mistake, but I was able and willing to start over and be the mother God made me to be.

Continuously working with the counselors at Glide, I went to the then Homeless Advocacy Project, a.k.a. HAP, on Sixth and Market Streets. I would go there when I had problems with my welfare, so I decided to go there to see what type of help I could get with visitations. I met with a representative, told them about my case, and they set me up with a family court attorney in the Financial District. I met this so-called family court attorney in the Financial District. I met with this woman. I was respectful, businesslike. I presented her with my letters, certificate, and other papers to let her know I was working hard and ready to resume being the mother I should've always been. She literally picked up my folder and threw it back at me. I looked at her, I looked around her office, then I looked back at her. I don't know how she read my look, then she picked up the folder and placed it neatly in front of me. Then she explained she doesn't fight for mothers like me, but she helped write the regulations that are counterproductive to mothers like me; in other words, she doesn't fight for family reunification but works with the system to keep families divided. It doesn't matter if the mother gets her life together and can prove she's capable of caring for her children. To myself, I was thinking, *What the heck am I doing here?* At that point, I gathered my belongings, thanked her for her time, which she didn't deserve at all, but like I said, I thanked her and left. And from where I sat, it was predominantly Black families headed by Black mothers who got shafted. Foster care in the community was big business.

I would find out about and attend family reunification workshops. At these workshops, they had family court attorneys, social service administrators, and family reunification social workers. I would meet these people, and they would take my hand—oh, I'm so proud of you. Then they'd say, "Call me," so I'd get their business cards, contact them with no return call, or the attorneys required money I didn't have. Family court attorneys, or at least in the mid-1990s, were not cheap, and most didn't do pro bono. I thought about this lousy scenario: if you're Black and you murder another Black person, you could get pro bono attorneys, but if you were a Black mother like me, then you're labeled as scum who didn't deserve to ever get her children back. There were a few Black women I knew of who were blessed enough to have caring CPS workers and court-appointed attorneys who helped get their families reunified. And believe me, they were few and far between.

While I was in the process of fighting for the right to have visitations on weekends and overnight with the girls in early 1997, I received a letter from the district attorney's office around March 1997 to pay child support. I went to court. The commissioner gave a continuance until after my upcoming graduation from City College. I felt like I was falling apart, but I stayed connected; I couldn't let this consume me. I used my connections: sharing with my counselors and at the 12-step meetings and finding help any way I could to deal with these problems. I really thank God for prayer because I needed it; now I'm fighting two cases: visitation and child support. "Whew, where is my fan? It's hot up in here."

It's around July 1997, I'm in child support court, and the assigned ADA, Paul, is assigned to my case. This man worked hard at giving me the blues. At the time, I was working as a "home care provider" at thirty hours per week, making about $175 per week. I was literally in court every two weeks. The ADA was confrontational and determined I was going to pay, not caring that my mother was caring for my children and she received cash aid and food stamps. I think this man had an opinion and perception that people like me were deadbeats. Period. After worrying about how I was going to pay money I didn't have, and the fear of possibly either being put in jail or losing what little I had (my apartment) just to pay child support, it was a week before the final showdown in court between myself and ADA Paul. I ended up in Moscone Park, literally in tears. I had to do something, but what? I felt like I was trapped because he was the ADA, so he had more power and clout over me. I prayed, I cried. I cried and I prayed. The solution was to go back to HAP to see about getting legal advice and legal representation. There wasn't much they could do to assist me because my daughters were in kinship foster care, but I was referred to the law library at Third and Market Streets in the Hearst Building. There, I met this older white guy who worked there, assisted me on how and where to look for child support cases similar to mine. He was really a blessing as well as a support system I needed. I was in court a week later; I went in secure and confident. There, ADA Paul, going on about me, and the commissioner, she was exasperated with him. Now it's my turn. I had my check stubs dating back from the last two months, along with my monthly living expenses, and the surprise presenting similar cases like mine from the law library. While I was making my presentation, the ADA literally turned his head around and asked me, "Where did you get that from?" I looked at the bench, then back at him, and responded, "The same place where you get your information from." I did have to pay child support, but at the time, it gave me the chance to look for more gainful employment in the child development profession since this is what my AA degree was in.

Continuing with seeking weekly visitations and overnights, I sought assistance at the legal advocacy project on Market Street. From there, I got a referral to an agency in the Women's Center located on Eighteenth Street in the Mission District. This is where I met this short Black woman. She was not afraid to stand up for what was right, and she knew what to do. She knew about my attorney. She could relate to what I was going through because she was once in my shoes. She assisted me in preparing a letter and referred me to a mediation program through a State of California agency located on Market Street between Van Ness Avenue and Franklin Street. I thanked her, and the following day, I contacted the agency and made an appointment to meet with a state representative at the mediation office. I met this Black woman; she was really helpful, treated me with respect and dignity, and she listened to me. She took the time to explain what "mediation" is and how they work to bring communities together. She let me know she was there to help me, and she would. She helped me prepare a letter for family court and child support court, so upon my next court date, I was able to give the letter to the commissioner, which resulted in the court granting the weekend visits along with prorating my child support payments since the girls were with me from Saturday morning to Sunday after Mass. From there, we'd head back to Momma's, then around five o'clock, I would leave from there to attend my Sunday evening 12-step meeting. *Note*: If you notice, I got my visits through child support court, a component of family court.

In early 2000, I received a letter from the SF District Attorney Child Support Bureau that I owed child support from January 1997 to May 1997, which was impossible since this matter was dealt with in family court in 1997. I took off work to report to the DA's office. I met with this investigator who never introduced himself, and he was a piece of work. I asked why I was being charged this back payment when at the time I was in school, and I had explained in family court, and the commissioner documented that the case would pick up after I graduated. Okay, case closed. Not. This investigator was a piece of work. He insisted that I owed this money and I would have to pay it. At this point, he sat back in his chair, crossed his legs, and that was when I said, "So this is how it is." His response: "That's pretty much it." Now I was playing dumb. I asked him the name of the person who headed the agency. He gave the name Milton Hyams, who was the acting director. As I was preparing to leave, I thought to myself, *I'm going to write a personal confidential letter to the acting director.* I went home and wrote a six-page letter to Mr. Hyams. I informed him the investigator was rude, unprofessional, and never even gave his name. Several weeks later, I received a telephone call from this woman from the city auditor's office. She asked, "What exactly happened?" I also told her about the encounter with this investigator; he refused to give me his name and how he reared back in his chair, letting me know I owed this money and there was nothing I could do about it. She really was supportive, then she dropped the bombshell. She said to me, after they completed an audit of my case, they owed me $1,100. I couldn't believe my ears. She explained the extra money I was paying to child support, so I could either get a check mailed to me or apply it to my child support case. I told her to send me my money.

I shared at meetings about my child support case. I shared that if they were like me, with money deducted from their paychecks and from income tax returns, along with paying out extra money, they should request an audit; they might have money due to them. Even today, if you're a nonviolent/noncustodial parent, you're a working productive member of society and you want to rebuild your relationship with your child/children, fight for your rights. If you have to pay child support, pay it. As time goes on, you may even be able to get your child/children in your custody. But whatever you do, do it right. Spend/make time with your child/children, be active in their education, attend extracurricular activities, discipline and teach your child/children, because they'll need it. That's how they learn. Teach them by setting the example of being responsible for their actions. Most of all, raise them to know the Lord God. That is the most important part of their development in every area of their lives.

By 2000, my two youngest daughters were still in school. By then, it got to the point where any day of the week we could meet. They would go to family reunions on their dad's side, and I even started going to their school functions. Sometimes it would just be Danielle, and Simone would catch BART over to my apartment in Oakland. They were responsible enough to bring JP, who was about two and a half. I loved taking care of my children; it was my job to care for them. I just wanted my right to a second chance at being a parent and doing it right that time around. I messed up, I got my life together, and I've kept it together. My house was clean, with plenty of food, in a safe and accessible area, and had good transportation. They knew the neighbors and the complex manager and her family.

Never give up on life; always share what you go through; give those resources, referrals, and network connections to others, because this is what life is all about. God gives and pours into each of his children, and therefore, we should pour into and give to others.

Born July 25, 1922, Died January 18, 1992. This is pops in a photo shoot in 1991, he was getting ready to make a jazz album

This is pops in WW2. United States Army 92nd Infantry, he received an honorable discharge after serving in Germany, Italy and North Africa

I Did It for Love

<blockquote>

No man can serve two masters; for either he will hate the one, and love the other; or else he will hold to the one, and despise the other. Ye cannot serve God and mam-mon.

—Matthew 6:24 KJV

</blockquote>

Working the steps with my sponsor, attending meetings and a workshop my sponsor turned me on to, I was forced to face my past. What led me to the state of addiction. What led me to a state of why I chose/ended up with having my children in my mother's care and me on the streets. As I thought about my past, this part took me back to 1982. I was twenty-five years old, just had my third child three months earlier, I was unemployed, living with my mother and two younger sisters (the youngest was in high school), in and out of college, and I found out I was pregnant, again. I told my boyfriend. I don't recall the conversation, but I ended up taking the route of an abortion, thinking everything would be okay or at least get a little bit better between me and him. The turmoil I faced in my life was to please this man of mine who didn't understand or support me, and I didn't understand him. It wasn't until several years into my recovery I realized our relationship was about sex, everything else was null and void.

My problem was, I wanted to be like other women who had live-in boyfriends. You know, have the nicest clothes, money in my pocket, and he would work while I stayed home and did nothing.

As I looked through the windows of my eyes, I saw what I wanted to see. I convinced myself to believe what I wanted to believe. When Bill came along and showed me the attention I was looking for, I took what he had to offer and totally confused it for love. One thing I can say is, he loved his children, and they definitely loved their dad. To this day, they still have a relationship with him; they look out for him. He would pick them up from school, babysat if needed, and he would always take them to visit their family.

As for me, I never took the time to be the woman I should have been. What I wanted to do and what I did were two different things. I lived on the outside of myself, always concerned about how others saw me. Even when my children were small, that voice in my head would tell me to leave. "Just take your children and leave." But I was weak, I was lazy, and I was mute. I always chose to look for and seek acceptance from others. This really affected me deeply because I was too busy being what I perceived motherhood to be. As long as I fed my children, bought them clothes, took them to church, and attended school meetings, I felt like I did my motherly duty. The truth be told, every time I had a baby, I got more stagnated, which eventually led me into the dark, seedy world of drug and alcohol addiction.

By April 1985, I had four children (one son aged ten, three little girls aged four and a half, three and a half, and thirteen months). It was still the same old scenario: no job, collecting welfare, and yes, unfortunately, still living at home with my mother. What is wrong with this picture? As I'm sitting here, typing with the Bible open in Genesis 3, it just occurred to me this particular scripture, Genesis 3:6, fit me well because that's exactly how I was when I got involved with him. He was that forbidden fruit that I bit into. I did it because I told myself he was just what I needed, he satisfied the physical and sexual of what I thought made the relationship. In the end, moving onto Genesis 3:7, it wasn't that we were both naked; it was my brain that was naked. It was my whole thinking process that left me naked, null and void. Totally and completely.

With the grand announcement of another unplanned pregnancy with four children, which left my better half, my parents, and myself unhappy with me. By now, my father stated his frustration and disappointment with me. Even though I was an adult, what parent wouldn't be concerned? He saw this whole scenario, and it stank (not stink); it stank like the devil's den. I went and got the abortion.

By now, it was 1987. Here I was, thirty-one years old, back in the same old boat, along with my cigarette/weed smoking, drug, and alcohol habit increasing. My crack addiction was out of control, and I was back at the OB-GYN, finding out I was pregnant with another child. I kept this baby, instead of taking care of myself and my baby by getting some help. My drug usage got out of control. I was so drug sick it never occurred to me that when I was using drugs, smoking weed, drinking alcohol and beer, so was my baby. The deception was, I ate and took my vitamins, but I failed to do the right thing: "Leave the drugs, alcohol, cigarettes, and weed alone." I did tell the doctor I was on drugs, so she documented it, but she never offered any type of help, yet I continued to keep my OB-GYN appointments.

When my baby was born, there were traces of drugs in her blood. She was taken from me and placed in intensive care. This was my first encounter with CPS (Child Protective Services). While I was in the hospital, I went to visit and hold her all day and all night. I would talk to her. I was released by Wednesday, so I stayed home during the day, then after the kids would go to sleep around midnight, I would head to Kaiser and stay with the baby all night. On Friday morning, the social worker, Mrs. W, who was really a nice and caring woman, came out to look at the house and talk with me. Since the kids and I were living with Momma, the social worker felt the environment was safe, and it was. She then contacted the hospital to release my baby to come home. She really wanted me to get myself together. She looked at me and said, using her hand (she positioned it straight), and said, "This is how a normal, adjusted life is." She held her hand straight, moved her fingers in a downward position, and said to me, "This is your life, and that needs to change." She gave me resources in the community to support me. One of the resources/connections was Mrs. K, a social worker at Sir Francis Drake Elementary School, now called Malcolm X Academy, in Hunter's Point, and she also referred me to meet with Brother J at All Hallows Rectory, along with attending meetings to get help for myself. She didn't want to separate the children from me. Since I was living with Momma, Mrs. W contacted the hospital to release the baby that day.

Still living at home, I would try to talk with Bill about getting custody of the kids. I told him he could get a place to live and I could get help for myself. Now either he just didn't seem to get it, or he didn't want the responsibility of being a single father. He would sarcastically tell me, "If you get into a program, so will I." But that was an empty promise he was incapable of keeping. Back to myself, the family court lawyer appointed to me was as dysfunctional as I was. I found out years later he was a drunk and didn't give a dead rat's tail about his clients. I was just another crackhead who didn't deserve my children, and he proved it with his lack of representation. Running back and forth to court was a waste of time. While attending the meetings, I saw Brother J sitting there. I thought to myself, *How could he help me when he needs help himself?* By now, it was July 1988, and my addiction was out of control. I was no longer cautious about my surroundings, which led to my first time getting arrested for drugs. By now, I had stopped attending the 12-step meetings. It surprised me that the CPS worker, my court-appointed attorney, or the courts didn't find out. By 1991, I had a probation officer, but it was basically just "Don't get caught with any drugs or paraphernalia."

Years later, I would have to hold myself accountable because, even though I got and stayed clean, the punishment was, the courts never reunified me with all four of my daughters. And by admitting that it was on me, it helped me move forward in my life. Joining church and learning to renew my relationship with God helped me forgive myself and let go. My children and family never stopped loving me; therefore, I had a lot to thank God for because he never gave up on me. Jesus continued to walk with me and carry me even in my worst of times as well as the good times. And that is a blessing in itself.

Sing unto the Lord a new song: sing unto
the Lord, all the earth. (Psalm 96:1–9 KJV)

Issues: They Just Keep Coming

God is our refuge and strength a very
present help in time of trouble.

—Psalm 46:1 KJV

It was the latter part of 1997 when I first started to deal with the emotional struggle of getting abortions. Around July 1997, I found out I was going to be a grandmother for the first time. It was quite a shock due to my daughter's age, and for some reason, abortion became a real big issue for me. It wasn't until this time that I realized there was another issue eating at me: abortions. That's because I had several of them. Through the years, I would wonder if they were a boy or a girl in each case. What would I have named them? These were empty questions for these babies that never got the chance to exist. I never discussed this part of me with anyone, not in my women's group or 12-step meetings; I didn't go to confession. I never thought it would come back at me the way it did. I did lose two babies, one in 1979 and one in 1985, so those were beyond my control. As for the abortions, I lived with those secrets for years. I did what I considered the unspeakable; I got rid of two babies in the name of love. I should've stood my ground and said, "No, I'm keeping these babies." I never realized that getting these abortions was emotional for me because these unborn babies were a part of me; aborting them was like killing a part of myself. When I hear the statement "It's my body, it's my choice," for me, it's more of a circumstance, and I think the average teen or adult female who gets an abortion has a reason behind it. Therefore, I can't knock or condemn them because their pregnancy can be a product of rape, incest, a married man, or deceit, but it's emotional and it's traumatizing.

It was the latter part of 1997 when I was watching this program. This man who hosted a television show talked about his young son who was murdered years earlier. He was asked if he ever wondered what his son would be like had he lived. The man responded that whenever he thought of his son, he only thought of him the short time he lived on this earth. I sat there, staring at the television with tears streaming down my face. I cried, because how could I have been so cold to get rid of my babies like that? It was no one's fault, not even my boyfriend's, because at the end of the day, the final decision came from me. I was so sorry for being so selfish and thoughtless. I asked for forgiveness, and I was able to let those two aborted babies go. Then I learned to forgive myself, and from there, I supported my daughters in their pregnancies because that's what they needed. My mother supported and prayed for her granddaughters during and after their pregnancies. You're fifteen, eighteen, nineteen, or twenty; you end up getting pregnant; your plans will definitely shift in a different direction because now there's a baby on the scene. It doesn't matter if the dad is around or you get married or you live at home—you can still achieve your dreams, especially in the twenty-first century; there are so many advantages and support systems.

Today, my personal opinion on abortion is "It's not about it's my body or it's my right." I learned to realize my body is a temple and it's a gift from God. The scripture 1 Corinthians 6:15–20 KJV makes it clear: "What? Know ye not that your body is the temple of the Holy Ghost which is in you" (verse 19), "For ye are bought with a price" (verse 20). That price is Jesus going to the cross for my sins.

As a Christian, I would say no to that female considering an abortion. I would help in any way I can with resources, referrals, and support, but I also realize for each teenage girl or woman, it's a personal decision. I would definitely pray for that woman or girl who has to make that decision. For me, I can say this, and I'm willing to bet there are other women like me who would agree: abortion is emotional. It leaves an inner scar for that woman to make the decision of getting an abortion.

We live in a world where people are constantly seeking sexual freedom to the point where we see, from the outside or in the Christian world, we call it carnal. Like me, I lived on the outside of myself, and although I was raised in the church, I blocked out, or I just didn't understand that I was special, I was special in God's eyes. I sought popularity; I figured if I lived like the people I admired or emulated, then all would be well. After I got clean, some of the people I wanted to be like were just as messed up as me. They fell into drugs and alcohol; several of my classmates from junior high school served prison time. But thank God, like me, they got themselves together. All I can say is, if you're looking on the outside of yourself, if you feel like you're alone, then start with God. Start by getting on your knees and having a conversation with God because he's waiting for you to do that. Even people who don't go to church or pray regularly still, at times, will ask God for his help, such as "Lord, help me get that promotion" or "God, if you're real, do this or do that" or "Please, God, help me." Start with abstinence; it can and will lead you to have that heart-to-heart conversation with God. God understands your position, but he's already mapped out the master plan for your life long before we're even thought of. God didn't make us to be alone; he created each and every human being with a purpose. The problem is our thinking, doing it our way; we think we know what's best for us. For me, free will got in my way because I interfered with God's business, but it was and is his grace and mercy that saved me, just like God's grace and mercy will save you. Be a living example before your children, teach them, talk with them, and listen to them. Most of all, pray for and with them daily.

To that man out there who wants to be a player trying and wanting to prove your manhood, ask that married man or the brother with multiple children by multiple baby mamas who has to pay child support for all those children. Don't get yourself into a position where you're telling a woman to get rid of your child because you don't want to be exposed or because you can't afford another child or you just don't want another baby. Every man can gain sexual freedom by giving his life over to Christ Jesus. Then you can free yourself from the need and myth of proving yourself as a man by how many women or girls you can lie down with. My father was a musician, but one thing we never heard our mother complain or get angry about was our father chasing women. My father had a full-time job at the post office, yet on any given night, he may have had a gig, and sometimes he would say to Momma, "Gloria, I have a gig. Do you want to come?" And she would say, "Yes." Even after their divorce, they would still go out with each other.

When I first moved here to Brooklyn and started teaching over on Rodgers and Clarkson Avenues, I was impressed with several fathers in my class who had full custody of their children. One little girl, Gabby—her mom worked nights, so the dad would bring her to school; he'd wash her hands and sit her at the breakfast table. I remember one occasion Gabby's father said during the weekend she wasn't feeling well and, if she appeared sick, to just call him and he would come to get her. At my current school, one of my former students, his dad would come around 3:15 p.m. to pick him up. He would stay, help put the kids' shoes on, set the snack table, and all the kids loved him, and so did Ms. C. and me.

Husbands, fathers, boyfriends, and even grandfathers do so many great things, and they're so amazing; we can't live without them. This is to all men of all nationalities: you don't have to play into the myth about manhood. Manhood isn't about a gun or selling dope. Manhood isn't about multiple women or baby mamas, along with the drama. It's about following what God has created you to be. Just because your dad wasn't in your life when you grew up doesn't mean you have to cut yourself short. One of the brothers at Acts Full Gospel spoke about his mother raising him and teaching him to have respect and dignity for himself, the women in his family, and most of all, God. Today, he's a loving father and husband, and he's giving back and continues to give back to boys aged five to twenty-one. My grandsons were in that support group, and it was a blessing for my grandsons and all the boys who were a part of that support group. They taught the boys how to tie a tie, took them to ball games and sports events, got signed permission to go to their school, met with their teachers and counselors, letting the school see these boys have the support of their community. The boys would raise money by washing cars. One Saturday, the boys were taken out to feed the hungry on Thirty-Second and San Pablo in Oakland.

Men, you don't have to do drugs; you don't have to drink alcohol or chase females. Instead, use your God-given gifts and talents, as described in Matthew 25:14–30 KJV. Remember, those myths are there to keep you in bondage, keep your self-esteem low, and always blame others for your problems. There are so many boys in the community, at church, at school, in juvenile hall, even in your family who need a positive male role model, and you're it. Also know that the same Jesus who died on that cross over two thousand years ago also died for you. He said in a parable that the temple would fall and rise in three days. Jesus is the temple that fell, and he rose on the third day. This scripture lets us know our bodies are temples, so treat your body with tender, God-given, agape love. "What? Know ye not that your body is the temple of the Holy Ghost…For ye have been bought with a price: therefore glorify God" (1 Corinthians 6:19–20 KJV).

To my soul sisters out there, take that deep breath, and ask yourself, "Is he really worth losing your self-respect for?" Are you willing, or can you afford, to neglect yourself and your children for him? Ask yourself if he loves you the way you love him. When a man truly loves you, he won't pressure or make you feel obligated to satisfy his own selfish needs, his wants, or his desires. He'll love and respect you. If you have children or you care for a sick or elderly relative, he'll take the whole package. He will honor and give God the glory ahead of anything in his life. And most importantly, he'll seek and value your opinion. He'll marry you in Jesus's name. "And the Lord said, it is not good for man to be alone" (Genesis 2:18 KJV).

Me and my four queens from left to right: Simone, Jawana, Rena, and Danielle. Taken on Saturday night, December 2017, before I moved to Brooklyn, New York.

My five grands from left to right: Darmarr Jr., Kaia, and JP in the back. Camielle, Monica, with Rena standing behind Monica.

My mother, Gloria when she was in high school in St Louis, Missouri.
This picture taken between 1941-1942. She was a devout Catholic who
helped the women in the neighborhood, she was stylish and smart

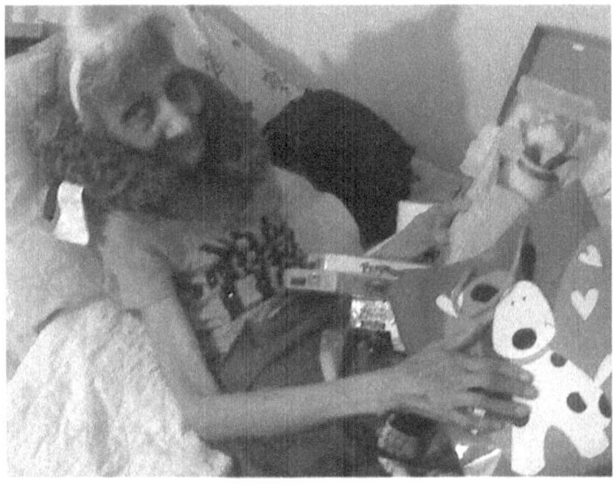

Here's Momma Gloria; she was known as Ms. Stith, Grandma,
Momma, and Aunt Gloria. She lived a full life. Sunrise: February 22,
1927; sunset: May 6, 2013. This was her eightieth birthday party.

Section 3

Start Taking Some Responsibility

Let all bitterness, and wrath,
and anger…be put away.

—Ephesians 4:31–32 KJV

Dear Father God,

Thank you for the everlasting, ever-loving patience you provide for me. Thank you, Father God. Because of you, I'm finally taking responsibility and charge over my errors. Because of you, I'm a better person today, and I feel better about myself and who I am. Thank you, Father God, always and forever in Jesus's mighty name.

John 1:1–5 KJV
Hebrews 11:1 KJV
Titus 2:3–4 KJV

Go for It

I will bless the Lord at all times; his praise
shall continually be in my mouth.

—Psalm 34:1 KJV

When we're born, our destiny has already been set by God. He has a task for each and every one of us on this beautiful green earth. Our God-given gifts and tasks connect us in one way or another. When I look back into my childhood, I had no idea that playing school or even the task of caring for my younger sisters or going to the store for Momma was setting my destiny in motion. What I desired and going for was a different story. Here is my journey that I'll call "Go for It."

In the past, there were reasons why I didn't go for it, reasons like fear of failing, fear of what others would say, fear of being snickered at, talked about, or criticized behind my back. I didn't think I was good enough, smart enough, dark enough, pretty enough; I lived in the projects or came from a certain family, choosing to use drugs and alcohol over reason and sanity. And most of why I would never go for it was that I didn't pray, didn't think about praying, and mostly didn't even give God the thought that if I took my concerns to him, I would have received help, gotten the word on what to do, and I certainly would've avoided a pathetic life as a drug addict / alcoholic.

Looking back on my life, as young as nine years old, my mom subscribed to magazines like *Ebony*, *Essence*, *Black Enterprise*, and she was a regular reader of *Jet Magazine* (also owned and published by the late John Johnson), *Look*, and *Life Magazines*. I would open up these magazines and see pictures of Dr. MLK Jr., Mrs. King, and their children. There were pictures of the turbulent civil rights movement, the war in Vietnam. At age eleven, Momma had a magazine solely dedicated to Dr. King after his assassination in Memphis, Tennessee, on April 4, 1968. As I turned each page, I carefully viewed each one, seeing Dr. King in the casket, a picture of his youngest child with her head on her mother's lap, watching the stilled photo of the Queen of Soul singing, pictures of his family, friends, civil rights pioneers, famous people, and politicians while anger and sadness went through my head. I wanted to tell my mother and father how I felt, but I just couldn't go for it. I came to the conclusion they would tell me to stop talking nonsense.

I hated the fact that people who stood and helped the Black community were brutally murdered like wild animals. To go for it for some was costly. As a child, I saw the images on television of Black men, women, teenagers, and children in the South being beaten and arrested; police would sic dogs on the protestors; and firefighters would spray water on the protestors as if they were putting out fires. All they wanted was to be treated as human beings. Have the right to eat where they wanted, go in any store they wanted. They wanted the right to vote; they wanted to represent their cities, towns, or neighborhoods. I swore when I got older, I was going to do something. I was going to make my voice heard, but then I would retreat, thinking there's nothing I could do. So I'd go back to my reality by turning off the television, go to the dinner table, or simply leave the room.

I carried the lack of "go for it" into my adulthood. Even in my relationship with my girls' father, there were times I truly wanted to tell him how I really felt about me and him, my dreams, what I wanted for us and the kids. I even wanted to know what he wanted for himself, for me and him, or even for our family. Instead of talking, I would imagine how our lives would be. Then there were times I wanted to pack up, bring my children, and leave. You know, go on my own, leave my mother, Bill, and just start over with me and the kids. Sometimes I would talk with my father about what I wanted to do; he would ask me how I was going to do it. "What about your children?" I would tell him I'll do it tomorrow or next week, and as a result, he'd end up telling me, "Victoria, you're always talking about what you're going to do." He would say to me, "You know what you are? You're a procrastinator." What is that? All talk and no action. I had no drive, no action, no start or finish. I never developed or wrote an action plan. What I had and what I needed to get to where I really wanted to go. The only "go for it" I had was smoking weed and drinking, which led me down a dark path of near self-destruction until July 11, 1994.

Effective January 1, 1989, I was on my own, with my parents raising my five children, aged eleven months to thirteen years old. The only "go for it" I had was survival mode. By 1993, I was going to Glide's Program, but I would drop out, yet it became a refuge for me. I would go there for breakfast, lunch, and dinner, sometimes spending the whole day in the Tenderloin, a.k.a. TL, meaning I'd go to the circle or go to the office to talk (more like dump) to the female counselors. But in all that complaining and still hitting the brick wall, I didn't realize I was going for it. A change was coming; I had people who looked like me who would listen to me. They didn't make fun of me. On Wednesday, July 13, 1994, I made my way to Glide for the 11:00 a.m. circle. This time, there was the opportunity to try outpatient again, but this time I decided to go for it. I signed my name on the dotted line. Big dreams, big goals, big plans.

As a kid, I never thought about how I would become a teacher, but I just wanted to do it. I loved being around people. Living a lifestyle that brought me to my knees, starting as a teen and young woman, going through bouts of depression in later years, I understood as a woman, a Black female with no confidence in myself, always accepting what others thought of me. The insecurity of growing up in the projects meant I could only dream, but to go for it wasn't for me. But going through the program at Glide gave me the confidence and determination to go for it. I attended those support groups, women's group, individual and group therapies, even if I held back or didn't tell everything. Attending 12-step meetings weekly and going back to church, I began to slowly love myself. I mean, I really truly loved myself enough to where I didn't, I wasn't, I refused to go back to a lifestyle that offered absolutely nothing but hopelessness, despair, and the strong possibility of an early grave.

I will always give props to Glide's church pastor at the time I was there. He was more than a preacher; he was an activist, and he believed in people like me who lost hope, stopped believing, or never believed in themselves, enough to say in that circle, "We'll love you until you learn to love yourself." The word in this place was "unconditionally"; this was the fuel I needed. I was like a dead car battery jump-started back to life. I can do this. I will go for it despite knowing my weaknesses and knowing I was subject to anything, at any moment, at any time. I chose to go forward, I made a promise to God, and for once in my life, I wasn't going back.

In May 1997, after graduating from City College of San Francisco, I got a little stuck in finding a job. So along with some other members at Our Lady of Lourdes, we formed the Parents Who Care program at All Hallows School. It was a place where the neighborhood children and teens could come to do their homework, play games, talk, and watch movies. There, I was introduced to this woman who worked for the SF Housing Authority. We started talking. I told her I graduated from CCSF with an AA in child development. She gave me the business card to call the director of a child development center in Potrero Hill projects. For the first several days, I kept looking at the card because I had a job lead, but I kept thinking, *What if.* My head said, "Call her. You won't know what the results will be if you don't call." I contacted the director, we set up a meeting, at the time I had just completed the application process to obtain my teacher's child development permit. The main question I had to answer was whether I had a criminal record, and the answer was yes. While pursuing employment as a teacher, I was also working on obtaining my child development teacher permit. This woman in the teaching credentialing, I guess, was assigned to me. It was a process; I didn't realize it then, but she was an angel sent from heaven. She would always reassure me by telling me, "Don't worry, we're going to pray about it." She spoke like a true Christian; she treated me as her sister in Christ Jesus. She let me know it didn't matter that I had been arrested on drug possession; what mattered was, I cleaned up my life, I was off drugs and alcohol, I had gone back to school and graduated, and I held stable employment for several years straight. I was trustworthy; my character and reputation became my bond and my word, and that's what counted.

By now, it's the spring of 1998, and I've just moved to Oakland, working in San Francisco's Potrero Hill neighborhood. I gotta tell you, God is beyond wonderful. I mean, I just can't give him enough props. He seriously and joyfully operates in the right place at the right time. (Just a quick notation: All Hallows and Our Lady of Lourdes were under one parish. There was some controversy among some parishioners that Lourdes was under All Hallows and vice versa. For me, it didn't make a difference because I grew up in All Hallows Church.) But anyway, I believe it was at Parents Who Care where I was talking to one of my All Hallows sisters. I told her I was applying for my teacher permit but I had also been arrested on possession charges. She told me to apply to get an expungement and to come down to the Public Defender's Office. So I was like, "Who do I talk to?" She said, "Me, I work there." I was thinking, *Get the heck outa here.* I applied and was granted the expungement on June 12, 1998; it happened so fast. I didn't even know who my PD (public defender) was. He looked at me with a smile and said, "Congratulations." I was like, "We're done?" He said, "Yeah. Bye."

From my first teaching position in 1997 in the State of California to my last hiring in 2015, I had to go through the exemption process. To show how good God is, I would always get hired, whether it was San Francisco, Oakland, Castro Valley, or Pleasanton, in the suburbs, the projects, or in between. I taught children of every walk of life, from low-income class to working class, to professionals such as lawyers, researchers, medical doctors, and RNs. I taught different nationalities from South Korea to interracial, Middle Eastern, suburban whites. When I look back, God took me from my comfort zone of San Francisco and Oakland to opening my mind.

In these twenty-eight years, nine months, and twenty-six days of sobriety, I worked daily to increase my faith, relationship, and total dependence on God. I feel like when I joined Acts Full Gospel COGIC in 2007, my walk in Christ Jesus grew. Being a part of the sisterhood, topics covered us as women, seasoned women were covered. The book of Titus 2:3–7 KJV, I now realize, also enabled and assisted my "go for it," teaching me to be supportive, a good listener, adviser, and gentle corrector to my daughters, my granddaughters, women, and girls younger than me and to carry myself respectfully, walk my Christian walk daily. Sometimes I may not always agree with what they say or do, but my obligation is to support them, pray with and for them, and most of all, show them that Jesus Christ is the only way.

By God's grace and mercy toward me, I've been able, since 1995, to make so many accomplishments, turn my dreams into realities. Has life been good in these last twenty-eight years? Not always. Some of my downsizes were due to my fault, not listening or doing it my way. I lost several jobs, went through two vehicle repossessions, about four evictions, yet I stayed clean and I stayed sober. By 2004, I started writing Gospel songs. By 2005, I got invited through my former boss and still friend to sing at church musical events. At first, I was a little nervous because I finally got to do what I wanted—sing. But I wasn't like my friend and the others. I didn't know a lot of these people; were they going to like me? Could I make people shout "Sing, Vickie"? No. What God did was, he opened my heart, and he gave me the tune, the lyric, and, more importantly, the message. By 2009, I started hosting gospel concerts at a church on Thirty-Seventh and Market Streets in Oakland. From there was the birth of Vicstar Productions. In 2010, bringing in my grandchildren with Jawana, Rena and Danielle's permission I was able to form God's Anointed Children.

As time rolled on, by 2016, I started listening to this radio station, Musical Rejoice Soul Food; they would advertise Christian Faith Publishing. At church, several friends and family members would say to me, "You need to write a book." Going for it doesn't mean you become filthy rich or you get every type of entertainment award there is. Going for it means doing what God planted inside you. It's that burning desire to write a book, take that trip to another country or across the US, to a state you've never been to before. Volunteer at church, your community, your child's school, or your favorite organization. Doing whatever your desire is, doing what God's desire is for you. I got accepted into Brooklyn College for the upcoming fall 2023 semester. I'm going to major in religious studies, and I have to add a second major, so I chose music. This past Easter/Resurrection Sunday, I was given the opportunity to be a part of the musical. I was asked to give a ten- to fifteen-minute sermonette about Jesus rising from the grave. I joyfully accepted, but then, a couple of days later, I was like, "Why did I commit to this?" But I had to realize this is not about me; it's about the message God wants me to convey. It's about the plan he has for me.

I've written one play and am working on another I'd like to perform. I don't care if I get paid for it or not; I just want to do it. I have written many more gospel/Christian songs, and for children, youth, and young adults as well, that will be performed. Every now and then, I do spiritual sermons on social media live. I've written one book, *Who Am, I Am*, and I'm working on this book now.

Even at my age and where I am today, life will not always be about the easy or comfortable way but the opportunity to push forward, you know, "go for it." The foundation my parents set, even in their challenges and obstacles, is what set the foundation for me. Even my past drug/alcohol addiction, homelessness, incarceration, and depression set a foundation for me, because in order to go for it, by going through this and getting the one-on-one and group therapy / support groups as well as 12-steps, I was able to face why I was incapable and unable to go for it.

I Took God 4 Granted

He that turneth away his ear from hearing
the law, even his prayer shall be an abomination.

—Proverbs 28:9 KJV

By the time I got to my third year in recovery, things were going well for me. I had my own place to live; my girls and grandson were visiting me in Oakland and staying the whole weekend. I was entering a new phase in life, and although I had to pay child support, move into a larger apartment, and work full-time, I felt like life for me was moving forward. What I didn't see, what I wasn't prepared for, was dealing with another inner demon in me: letting go of resentment, petty anger, and abandonment issues.

In the fall of 1997, I got the teaching position in Potrero Hill. I was assigned to work with three- to five-year-olds. We had four teachers and twenty-four children in the classroom. We worked well together. Once a month, she had the parents come and clean the center, including the cots their children slept on. The site director was a Black woman who fought against adversity, and she went from a high school–dropout teen mom to a mother on welfare to teacher's aide to becoming site director, an advocate for the union, workers' rights, especially for her staff. Yet she had a tendency and a knack for being beyond straightforward; in other words, she could be intentionally insulting. Instead of me asking what she meant, trying to learn from her, or even correcting myself, I developed a resentment against her. It wasn't her who did or said anything wrong or offensive to me.

I took it that way because I didn't like to be corrected. This is the woman who fought to get me this teaching job because she believed I deserved a second chance, and instead of taking advantage of job and educational opportunities, I got mad and quit in August 1998, right after the children's graduation.

She was like my counselors and the executive director at Facts on Crack. They would say things to me or tell me things to help me look at how to improve my life, what I could use, and what I could get rid of. Instead, I got mad; I got insulted because she wouldn't see it my way. She didn't stroke my victimization. In my early recovery, going to therapy, I wasn't always honest; I didn't tell my part because I wanted to be the victim—you know, "poor, poor me." Although I attended 12-step meetings, did service, attended church, sang in the choir, I even prayed, but I didn't pray to God in a sincere way. When I prayed to God, I didn't pray asking him to give me strength to deal with life, let go of resentments, and stop blaming others. I didn't do what my sponsor suggested: writing those "dear God" letters and getting deep into my real issues. From there, I continued to make mistakes, I acted on impulse, and therefore, I continued to run away from good jobs. I even began to fail in my classes at San Francisco State University because of going into avoidance mode, inner unjustifiable anger, and harboring secret grudges. This part of my recovery took me years to work on.

Although my basic needs were falling apart, I continued to attend church regularly, sing in the choir, and also serve as a lector. I refused to break away from God, but I got desperate. I started watching different televangelists talk about prosperity. My church home at that time was Our Lady of Lourdes; I sang in the choir and was a lector. I started watching televangelists, and they spoke on prosperity, so my prayers became more money-oriented. Then there was the catchphrase "name it and claim it," but that didn't seem to work for me. My prayers became "I need money, give me a husband." I would pray that God would make my MK business grow. My prayers were "gimme, gimme, gimme." What I failed to do (whether it was intentional or not) was pray a prayer of gratitude for getting hired or anything God gave me or blessed me with. I didn't pray to God, thanking him for my family, that my children and grandchildren loved me and looked up to me. Going through these turbulent times from 2002 to 2006, I didn't journal about it. I didn't call my sponsor or my friend D, because they would show me my part and ask me what's really going on. In other words, they wouldn't see things *my* way, or at least that was my perception.

The biggest reason was, I just didn't want to hear the truth. The truth was, I had flaws; I just wanted to smooth things over, I wanted it to be my way, I wanted to be right, and most of all, I wanted to be the victim—you know, feel sorry for *me*. Not working this part of my program, from 2002 to 2006, God provided just enough for me to live. In this time period, I had two vehicles repossessed, and I faced five evictions where I agreed to move. I kept coming up short, but I never stopped going to church, never stopped praying, and never stopped singing in the OLOL and Nor Cal GMWA choirs. I continued to keep my promise to God: I never went back to drugs, alcohol, or prostituting myself.

By January 2006, I lost my teaching job in Livermore, California. I had a nice one-bedroom apartment on MacArthur Boulevard in East Oakland. The way I lost that apartment was this: in August 2005, I had fallen a month behind on my rent, so when I got the job in Livermore, instead of paying up the delinquent rent, I purchased a vehicle. Listen closely, instead of me praying a prayer of thanks for God blessing me with this job, I saved up the money and purchased a Ford Taurus. It was a sour deal. I went to a dealership on Park Boulevard in Alameda, California. The first price was $8,888.88. When I went back three days later to pay the down payment and sign the contract, it was marked up to $13,000.00. I should've walked away from the deal. But I dealt with those shady dealers instead.

City College of San Francisco Graduation Class 1997. Proud me with my associate arts degree. I completed my dream successfully. Wow.

In February 2006, I ended up living at a Christian Women's Home in East Oakland. It was owned and operated by an evangelist who attended Acts Full Gospel COGIC, and her sister was the house manager. I found out about this Christian group home when I attended Acts instead of Lourdes that Sunday. There was an information board in the church's lobby where I saw an advertisement. I contacted the church, and they referred me to Evangelist M, who worked with me so I could continue to attend Nor Cal rehearsals and functions. I was thanking God for this Christian women's home. It was a place of safety, godliness, and cleanliness, and there wasn't going to be any mess because both of the sisters wouldn't have it. Thank God for that. I was angry and upset with myself for getting into this mess. It was in this place that I became humble. God always knows how to work things out. He provided a private time where I was able to pray and ask God for his forgiveness toward me. I mean, seriously prayed for God's forgiveness. I was really sorry because I looked at all my losses in recovery and realized I didn't have to go that route. From there, doors began to open for me.

During my time at the women's home, I got my joy, incentive, and determination back. It was time to be productive again.

This refuge was meant not to be permanent but to be a hand up. I started by seeking employment and saw a position at a private school in Pleasanton, California, looking for a toddler teacher. I called the school and got an interview. The teacher I was replacing and her husband were missionaries moving to the South Pacific Islands for full-time missionary work. I was contacted and asked to volunteer in the classroom for several hours, then invited back the next day. After that, I was called into the office and offered the job because they liked how I never complained and followed directions. I was only on the job for six months; it was a good environment, but I needed to be where I could grow. By July 2006, I started another job search. In mid-August 2006, while in Dallas, Texas, I got a call from San Francisco Head Start for an interview. Two days after the interview, I was invited for a second interview. To make a long story short, my employment with SF Head Start lasted from September 15, 2006, to May 31, 2013, as a family advocate.

I will tell anyone never to take God for granted. God will always do what he says, though it may not be what you want or when you want it. Taking God for granted and not appreciating it only personified my hardheadedness. God probably thought, *Vickie, you seem to have all the unreasonable answers, so I'll just sit back. Call me when you're ready to show some gratitude.* Today, with my past experience, my spiritual growth, and navigating among unknown waters, I can fully trust in God. Even in messy situations, I find a way to show my gratitude and thanks to God.

Counselor 2 Advocate

And that ye study to be quiet, and to do your own business, and to work with your own hands, as we commanded you; that ye may walk honestly toward them that are without, and that ye may have lack of nothing.

—1 Thessalonians 4:11–12 KJV

One of the things I noticed once I got clean was that there were recovering addicts and alcoholics working in the field of mental health and recovery. Upon my graduation from the nineteenth generation, I signed up for Aftercare, an extension of the program. At times, I was given responsibilities such as facilitating the 11:00 a.m. circle and attending some staff meetings. To know that I could be born, baptized, and raised Catholic, then convert to Pentecostalism and still know I'm the "workmanship of God," and to know that I can love and respect others' choices of how they live and worship God, is empowering. "For we are his workmanship, created in Christ Jesus unto good works, which God hath before ordained that we should walk in them" (Ephesians 2:10–18).

By the time I gained three years in recovery, I realized I had gained more than I even knew. Having gone through several years of therapy (group and individual) and reentering City College of San Francisco in August 1995, I completed my AA degree in May 1997. The same program I graduated from gave me the opportunity to facilitate the eleven o'clock group two or three times a week, which was interesting and different because now I was giving input instead of just receiving it. To help others, I had to be an example of working my program and living life on life's terms, along with staying clean. I still needed to check in, go to my 12-step meetings, work those steps, meet with my sponsor, and most importantly, rebuild my relationship with God.

January 1998 was life-changing for me. I entered my second semester at San Francisco State University, and at forty-one years old, on January 22, 1998, I became a grandmother for the first time. With a new grandson and my girls growing up, I had to take another step. In March 1998, with my growing family, I left the comfort zone of the Arlington Hotel and moved into my own apartment in Oakland. On June 12, 1998, I was granted an expungement by the Superior Court of the City and County of San Francisco. In September 1998, I ran into a friend I used to get high with. It turned out she and her sister had gotten clean. I told her I was job searching, and she told me to go see her sister at the People's Connection Temp Agency. Not long afterward, I got a work placement at the Pacific Stock Exchange, where I keyed in the end of the day's trading. This position taught me the importance of timely documentation. Although I worked seven hours a day, I needed a more secure full-time job to make sure my bills and child support were paid on time.

I started searching the want ads and found a counseling position in Oakland. It was a twelve- to eighteen-month in-patient program for pregnant women and women with children up to five years old. There were three houses named after inspiring women: one after Helen Keller and two after Winnie Mandela. There was also the Women's Center, a day treatment located on Forty-Eighth Avenue and International Boulevard, and eventually, a transitional house in West Oakland for graduates and their children to start living productive lives.

I thought this was just the job I was looking for. I could help these women. I telephoned the agency, and they scheduled me for an interview. The following week, I met with the assistant director. By the time the interview was over, I was offered a position at Mandela House 2. This was perfect because it was literally a four-block walk from where I lived. What made it even better was that it was a Black-owned business. The founder/CEO, a Black woman blessed by God herself, had never done drugs or been an alcoholic. Concerned and alarmed that so many Black women were crack-addicted and losing their children to the system, she was able to open a women's center on Forty-Eighth Avenue and International, along with three houses named in honor of Winnie Mandela and Helen Keller. In some of these cases, the siblings were separated and placed in foster care in different counties, which in my opinion made it intentionally difficult when these mothers had visitations. At least 75 percent of the women in the program were CPS (Child Protective Services) cases.

My job was a four-block walk from where I lived, which was great. I walked into that program all gung ho. I was excited and ready, and I just knew that my presence would make all the difference. I'd share my story, letting them know not to worry, all would be well. It was like I had all the answers, but I didn't. It bothered me that I wasn't getting through to the women. What also made things worse was that the first house manager wasn't welcoming toward me, so I had to do the best I could with the women. On Fridays, the houses would go to the women's center. One Friday, the house manager was outside the center and slipped, fell on the street corner, messed up her ankle, and never came back to work. On the real, that was fine by me. The manager of the women's center became Mandela House 2's house manager, which we (staff and women) were all glad about. Yet it still took me about the first three months on the job before I was able to really begin a relationship with most of the clients.

With the staff and house manager supporting me yet letting me know the focus needs to stay on the clients, I had to follow the same approach I was taught when I studied child development at City College: simply stop and listen to each woman who comes in to talk. Just like my story, each of these women had their own unique, near-tragic story. A story that weighed on them, a story they had to get out of their system, a story to the point it's either live or die. Working in a Black female-owned and dominated setting helped me stay clean and focused and understand even more the real need in our community. As Black girls and women, we were and still are ignored and demonized, and the only way for us to grow is to overcome our pitfalls through supporting one another, advocating, voting, going back to school to fulfill our destiny, claiming/reunification with our children, and growing spiritually ourselves and our households. Acts 16:30–31 says, "And he brought them out and said, 'Sirs, what must I do to be saved?' And they said, 'Believe on the Lord Jesus Christ, and thou shalt be saved, and thy house.'"

In August 2006, while Monica and I were in Dallas, Texas, at the GMWA National Convention, I applied for a teaching position with San Francisco Head Start. While in Dallas, I got a response via email asking me for an interview. I called and told them I was in Dallas but would be home by Saturday, so the interview was scheduled for the following Monday. I was told by the agency they found me a better fit for Family Advocate due to my work and education experience. Several days after the interview, I received a telephone call that the Family Advocate manager liked me. I worked for SF Head Start for six years and eight months. Whereas the families in treatment mainly struggled with drugs, alcohol, abuse, sexual trauma, and CPS cases, in Head Start I worked with families who struggled with noncitizenship status. They, too, wanted the best for their children and wanted to live the American dream, and it was my job to help them achieve those dreams in several key ways. Family Assessment basically involved asking questions around health, mental health, childcare, social services, adult education/literacy, and volunteering. IFPA was about goal setting. As the center's advocate, I met with the parents/caregivers quarterly with the goal to be accomplished by the third and final quarter of the school year.

When I first started working as a family advocate, it was kind of rocky because it was my first encounter working with undocumented and non-English-speaking families. I learned how to communicate with those who could speak a little English and how to utilize the language bank for parent committee meetings, parent workshops, and one-on-one sessions with each family. Learning to work with the mental health interns was challenging because I was a know-it-all; I tended to be overbearing and based issues and concerns on my personal intake. The truth was that they were educated and trained, with resources on how to deal with children and families who were developmentally delayed, had mental health and behavior issues. I had to learn to listen to what they were saying and how I could be effective in working with the parents to help their children by getting the services they needed, whether it was confidential counseling or services in their home language.

By the time the school year 2010 rolled around, I saw myself growing in the area of serving and understanding the families and working as a team player with the Head Start staff and support staff. I started getting along with the staff, and the families began to trust and confide in me more. This was because I began to understand their plight in the areas of immigration, work, and education. I saw our similarities in Black people, Latinos, Pakistanis, Samoans, and Asians in the areas of family, faith, education, and hard work. I saw families, whether they were American-born, were here on visas, had resident status, or even those who were classified as undocumented, all wanted and had the desire to rise. By holding myself account-able, I opened the door to be an asset to each and every family. My committed goal was to do everything I could to assist, support, and complete their goals with them. My goal was to do my job the best I could, meaning I had to get out of "my way" and "my head."

Quality Childcare

> But Jesus said, Suffer little children, and forbid them not, to come unto me: for of such is the kingdom of heaven.
>
> —Luke 18:15–17 KJV

In the twenty-first century, the quality of childcare has reached new heights. Technology allows for documentation in databases, and young children as young as two years old are able to have computer time, selecting age-appropriate stories, numbers, shapes, and alphabets. As for the staff, we're able to send out blasts to eight to twelve families at a time. With templates, it eliminates hours of writing weekly/monthly curriculum and other center- or classroom-related documentation. Since the pandemic, teachers and former teachers, like myself, were able to conduct in-person and virtual class participation. As for parent involvement, we develop weekly/monthly newsletters and give them the chance to seek basic need referrals, set up appointments and job interviews, or even take online classes.

Unfortunately, in the twenty-first century, striving to obtain permits and degrees in the early childhood education field is becoming difficult. My encounter in 2019 of getting denied into the Brooklyn College ECE Master's Program because of my GPA at San Francisco State University left a bitter taste in my mouth. It also kept on the forefront of what childcare is, especially in education and classroom qualifications, but how it affects teachers in the classroom. Are we teaching? Are we as classroom teachers getting the support we need?

Are we spending too much time doing paperwork? Do I really need a master's degree to change diapers and wipe noses? When I do fieldwork and I'm employed in the classroom, do I really have to give up my job for six months? It's these types of questions that are causing some ECE teachers to leave the classroom. I was listening to one of my favorite radio talk show hosts in early 2022; he stated that in 2021, over one hundred thousand ECE teachers left the field due to dissatisfaction in the classroom.

What do parents expect or view as quality childcare? Parents/caregivers want to know and expect that we know what we're doing. I'll answer this in several ways as a parent as well as an ECE professional. My experience as a parent began in 1977 when I got a summer job at Presidio Army Base. Because Mikey was only two years old and in diapers, I had to pay out of pocket, something like fifty per week. It was a center-based childcare owned by a Black couple who themselves had two children. They were really nice and would have the children color, say their alphabets and numbers, and take the toddlers on community walks. But I also knew I had to toilet train him because I couldn't afford to continue to pay out of pocket since my job was only for the summer. For the record, up until the early 2000s, if your child was 2.6 years old and toilet-trained, they could start preschool. In early 1978, Mikey was accepted into Audrey L Smith Child Development. From 1978 to 1980, the school served dinner from 5:00 p.m. to 5:30 p.m. where the parents were able to sit with their children and have dinner. ALSCD had a full-time social worker who was a Black woman, so she could definitely relate to the community, the challenges, and the issues some of us parents had. The center also connected us as parents, matching the families according to where they lived. Our children were taught about our culture through dance and story time, and whenever other holidays like Cinco de Mayo or Chinese New Year were celebrated, the children/families were served Mexican and Chinese dishes. The curriculum was implemented in a way that, for instance, in the month of February, which is Black History Month and when Chinese New Year is celebrated, the letters *B* and *C* are implemented, and it's the year of the rabbit. Science is included: what color is a rabbit, and how many feet does it have? How many ears does it have? The children watch a two-minute video on how rabbits walk then pretend to be rabbits. As an art project, the children color their rabbit ears then glue them onto their headbands to wear in the classroom.

I was working at an ECE program in Livermore, California, right before Thanksgiving 2005, in the preschool section where there was a luncheon for the children and their parents. I thought it was nice to have a Thanksgiving luncheon, but I was told it was a family-style meal. The school did not use the word "Thanksgiving" due to it being a religious holiday. As far as I was concerned, an entire curriculum had been erased because somebody (or somebodies) wanted to say that this holiday is religious. The surviving Pilgrims probably did pray that they survived. This was about the harvest, but it was also about two groups of people, two different cultures, coming together, which shows that they are thankful, they are sharing, they are giving, and that's what Thanksgiving is all about.

"The event that Americans commonly call the 'first Thanksgiving' was celebrated by the Pilgrims after their first harvest in the New World in October 1621. This feast lasted three days and was attended by 90 Native American Wampanoag people and 53 surviving Pilgrims of the Mayflower" (from Wikipedia).

What I love and feel quality childcare is when children are taught about other cultures in a way that they understand. Introduce them to foods that different cultures eat such as during the month of May, which is the celebration of Cinco de Mayo, as well as Mother's Day, also any children and teachers. Every month has something special, along with birthdays of children and classroom staff. I've worked in schools where we posted the staff with their pictures along with the month and day they were born.

Quality childcare was the relationship we had because most of the teachers and parents knew each other; we were community-based. Quality childcare at that time was having professionals and staff that looked like the people in the community, Black social workers to help and assist families, especially around special education, family issues like divorce, domestic violence, job training leading to permanent employment. At Grace Child Development, the parent meetings met once a month around 5:30 or 6:00 pm. They usually lasted an hour. Meals were provided for the parents along with childcare for the children who were still there. We had parent workshops on parenting, child development, volunteering, and issues that affected families in general. After the meeting, parents would also assist the cook, childcare, and cleaning up after the meeting/workshop.

As a childcare teacher, family advocate, and residential counselor, I'm constantly having to work on myself because working with children/families along with center and agency administration can be very challenging at times. For me, most of the time, the children are the less challenging because, working with them, they learn through play, social interaction, and repetition. They look forward to the different activities along with becoming independent through learning self-care: handwashing, brushing their teeth, going up and down the stairs / holding on to the banister, weening from the bottle, sippy cups, and diapers. One thing about young children up to five years old, when they learn, they master it, they are proud of what they can do. They express in the way what they can do.

As an active Christian attending church, Bible study, and Sunday School, along with reading daily spiritual affirmation, it's a constant reminder of what I need to do, especially in the area of raising children. I found out through reading the Word that as a teacher, I share the same responsibility in caring for and teaching children. I've also made mistakes in the classroom or would become irritable with the children, their parents, and at times other staff, site, and agency administrators. It was those moments I would say, "I'm not coming to work tomorrow." I want to quit or not show up, but I couldn't/can't because, like then and even on this current job, I keep showing up. I had and have learned to pray and think about professional, life, or spiritual key important points brought out in church sermons, Bible scriptures, and/or parent workshops on self-care.

In order for me to do the best I can in assisting quality care in childcare or even a residential setting, my attentiveness, my attendance in showing up every day is important because the children can become deeply affected when that familiar face is not in the classroom. Attending workshops on relationships with parents/caregivers as well as the children and supervision. Applying what I learn in the classroom. Using my life, work, and educational experience when working with the parents/caregivers, continuing my education and at the same time being an encouragement to other teachers, especially those who will be teaching for the next twenty to thirty years in this field.

Part II: How "Quality Childcare" Should Be Implemented"

Quality childcare begins with parent responsibility and parent advocacy. "Train up a child in the way he should go, and when he is old, he will not depart from it" (Proverbs 22:6 KJV).

Quality childcare means accessible childcare within walking distance from the family's residence or near the parent's/caregiver's place of employment. It should also be available in neighborhood elementary schools, churches, and recreation centers that have the space and can meet the DOE, DOH, along with other local, state, and federal guidelines for caring for children.

Quality childcare involves lowering the child-teacher ratio; as of now, for two-year-olds, the ratio of child-teacher is six to one—meaning, for every six children, there is one teacher. That's a lot for one teacher. For two-year-olds, the ratio should be one teacher for four children. Currently, for three- to five-year-olds, the ratio is two teachers per seventeen children; the ratio should be two teachers, one paraprofessional, and a teacher in training per seventeen children.

Quality childcare includes parent-caregiver inclusion, creating a parent-caregiver committee that meets monthly to discuss fund-raising and events, offers ECE parenting classes and opportunities to step into this great field. Note: during my family-advocate days at Southeast Head Start, there was one father who served two tours in Iraq and was diagnosed with PTSD. He would talk with us about his child's education, attend the meetings and parent workshops, and was voted by other parents as parent committee rep, then elected president of the Parent Policy Council.

Quality childcare provides all teachers, family advocates, office and maintenance staff the opportunity to become unionized just like K-12 public education teachers.

Quality childcare requires that when owners of private childcare centers decide to close their centers down, they must give at least sixty to ninety days' notice to staff and families, offering every kind of assistance to families in finding childcare replacement, along with assisting staff with job placement elsewhere and providing reference letters.

Quality childcare offers tuition and textbook financial incentives for childcare teachers, teaching assistants, and teachers' aides in earning their teacher certification/credentials.

Quality childcare allows teaching staff the opportunity to advance within the company.

Quality childcare provides family advocates with educational opportunities in areas such as social work, teaching, or administration, along with tuition, transportation, and textbook incentives.

Quality childcare ensures that all centers are fully equipped with all the supplies needed, including food/liquids to accommodate every child and classroom teacher who have food and dairy allergies. The City of Oakland Head Start provided every child, teacher, and staff with food and liquid substitutes.

Quality childcare involves teachers and parents working together to observe children's growth cognitively, in fine to gross motor skills, language, and social-emotional development. In 2020, I had two little boys at 2.10 years who were able to put together twenty-four-piece puzzles. When they were finished, they would stand next to the puzzle and look at their work.

Quality childcare means knowing what's wrong with your child. Children can have negative behaviors due to poor dental hygiene (cavities), poor vision, poor sleeping habits (tiredness), delayed speech, developmental delay, domestic violence, food allergies, drug/alcohol usage, or if parents/older siblings have undiagnosed mental health issues. Note: this is why we must work as a team. The classroom staff needs the support of the center director, center-assigned mental health specialist, and local, state, and federal elected officials.

Quality childcare ensures parents/caregivers attend mandatory parent orientation two weeks before the new school year begins. This gives them the opportunity to learn about the center, its operations, who the center director is, the center administrative/office staff, kitchen staff, and all the teachers. They will also learn about the role they can and will play in their child's/children's education. Also, they will have the opportunity to become involved in parent committees and advisory committees: education, health and nutrition, special needs, mental health, and community partnership. Informing parents/caregivers of dates and times to meet to have a "family assessment and goal setting plan," and if an interpreter is needed, arrangements could be made at the time of their assessment.

Quality childcare involves ECE schools with board members having at least two teachers included on the board. In decision-making and making changes that will definitely affect the teaching staff, having teachers on the board is an asset, because when an issue affects teachers, these teacher board members can bring back to the teachers for their input.

Quality childcare is more than universal childcare or building more ECE centers; it's also offering careers to the most important person that keeps these centers functioning: "the teaching staff."

Quality childcare vs. quantity childcare goes hand in hand. We need both. We need more childcare with before- and after-school service to accommodate the families we serve. I remember when my little sister was in nursery school back in 1969, and when my son was in preschool from 1978 to 1980, as well as when my girls were in childcare, there was before- and after-school care to accommodate their older siblings and former childcare/preschool students. Before- and after-school care is sorely needed to help families maintain their independence. It also provides part-time/full-time jobs and is great for internships for students entering into education, social work, health care, or any semiprofessional or professional field serving children from birth to seventeen years old.

Quality and quantity both matter; we need more Blacks, minorities, and men who represent the makeup of our families, as well as in administrative, decision-making, and policy-making positions. Many fellow teachers feel, as I do, that those at the top in policymaking, decision-making, and administrative roles have never set foot in a classroom or worked around Blacks and other minorities. I worked for schools in NYC and the Bay Area where ethnic foods and celebrations were excluded. June is Black Music Month and Juneteenth. For children's music, we can introduce Ella Jenkins, whose music can be used for large/gross motor skills, social/emotional development, and language. For Juneteenth, especially for older students from fourth to twelfth grade, and particularly for Black American students whose roots are from Texas, we can use role-playing, discussion groups, and art.

February hosts two celebrations: Black History Month and Chinese New Year (and did you know that South Koreans celebrate a similar festival to Chinese New Year?). We can read books to our young children written by Black and Chinese children's authors. When I was teaching in Castro Valley, California, for Chinese New Year, we did a great project with the children using eight boxes to make a dragon allowing all the children to participate. We incorporated large motor skills, cognitive development (art and math), language, and social/emotional learning. Teaching the words "Chinese New Year," we also taught the children and teachers "Gung Hey Fat Choy." It breaks down racial barriers and builds racial unity among everyone. In NYC in October, we celebrate Columbus Day. Despite the negative descriptions of Christopher Columbus, we can focus on the fact he was born in Genoa, Italy, and implement geography with a world map or globe. For Venice, Italy, children learn that residents and visitors travel in boats called gondolas and the drivers are gondoliers. Every example I've described is a lesson plan, including letters *B, M, H, C, N, Y, V, I, C, G* of the day or the week.

The lack of quality care creates extra work for teachers and is frustrating for parents/families who need the service while they work or attend school. It also leads to job burnouts, unnecessary absences, and abrupt resignations. Building teacher-parent relationships and providing monthly professional development for teaching staff assures parents/caregivers that their children will be in capable hands, providing nutritious meals, age-appropriate curriculums, social-emotional development, and assisting children who require various types of on-site services, thereby minimizing teacher burnout.

Note: When I use the term "services," I am referring to children who qualify for speech therapy, occupational therapy, inclusion, and behavior therapy.

Help Your Child

Train up a child in the way he should go:
And when he is old, he will not depart from it.

—Proverbs 22:6 KJV

As a parent, teacher, and child of God, I learned it's my duty to train up children according to God's Holy Word: Ephesians 6:4, Proverbs 13:24, Deuteronomy 6:7 KJV. Although we're made in God's image (Genesis 1:26–29 KJV), we are not perfect creatures; there is no such thing as the perfect and sinless human being. I learned to be grateful to God and realized the importance of these scriptures because they are the first guide in raising and teaching our children to grow and become what God has created them to be, even if they're born with behavior issues, speech, or physical disabilities. Your child, my child, our children—we all are born with a purpose in this world. Think of Moses; he stuttered, yet God used him, and God put him out front to lead the Israelites out of Egypt. Our current president, number 46, stuttered as a child, but with his mother's undying love and being his greatest advocate, as you can see, the president has grown to overcome his stuttering. Then there are people who will always have delayed speech, and there will be children who grow into adulthood with autism, Down syndrome, and other developmental delays. But with parents/caregivers seeking guidance, advocating for their child/children, and putting aside their own denials and ignorance, no matter what, their children can and will grow to make contributions to their lives and society.

When each and every single child is born, even if they're an identical twin or triplet, they will have their own unique makeup, fingerprint, footprint, and DNA. By four months, babies are learning to roll over onto their stomachs, kicking their legs, cooing. By five to six months, infants position themselves to crawl, to sit up, to laugh, to play/interact with those around them, and gurgle (baby talk). What a joy that by that time most babies are showing social signs and movement by six months. You say or think, "Thank God my baby is healthy."

The reality is, some infants don't live to see their first birthday. Infants as young as eight months show signs of neurological issues. Children are born with rare diseases; they'll never walk on their own, they're born or go blind and deaf, they have cerebral palsy, spina bifida, diabetes, heart disease, or even cancer where they lose a limb or are constantly in and out of the hospital. Those parents of children like these have probably asked God, "Why, why my child?" "My husband / baby daddy didn't do drugs, drink alcohol, smoke cigarettes or weed." "We attended all of our prenatal appointments and took classes." But this happens.

Immediately when I began my career in childcare in 1997, there were challenges. I fooled myself because I felt like because I changed my life, I no longer had this irrational thinking. I mean, on the real, for years, my brain had been soaked and saturated in drugs and alcohol. So believing that everything and everyone around me was going to be "okey dokey" despite what my counselors told me, what I heard in the rooms or even at church was a stretch. I needed to believe, I had to believe, and I wanted to believe that people were changing; we were in a different time—the nineties. In fact, I was even told, "This is the nineties, and this is the way it is."

Don't get me wrong, teachers are the greatest, and they leave a long-life impact on their students, which is why some of them grow up to be teachers, social workers, and family advocates. Generally, people who enter into these professions are called to this, but it's human error that gets in the way. I mean, every so many years, on some televised award show, a teacher will be selected to have their fifteen minutes of fame, walk among the stars, receiving an award for their lifetime duty, even given a check not for their own pocket but to purchase more supplies for the children they teach/mentor.

When I was a Head Start Family Advocate in San Francisco, I had a parent whose twin daughters needed to get an assessment for speech. As a single mother of three, she worked hard to care for all three of her children. We had a team meeting with her because she needed all the support she could get. In the team meeting, it was me, the center director, the mental health specialist, and their teachers. She consented to the evaluations, and they were qualified for speech therapy. I'll never forget, it was the middle of the day before we had the team meeting when she started crying because she wasn't a drug user, and there was fear and confusion about why this was happening to her girls. I thank God for allowing me to be there to comfort and reassure her that all would be well. I told her that getting help for them now is so important; by the time they get to the third or fourth grade, their speech will be clear, as if they never had a speech problem. When they transitioned from Head Start to kindergarten, their services continued. She was at an advantage and learned to advocate for her children.

We had a little boy, aged four and a half, who began to display signs of depression and mood swings. Unfortunately, the father of this child, in my professional opinion, intervened and deliberately refused help for his son. This child would uncontrollably run around the classroom; when his teachers asked him to use his walking feet, he would stop running, then, out of the blue, start crying, with tears streaming from his eyes. First, the center director and I met with his mom, then with both parents, to discuss what was going on. You could literally feel the tension between the child's parents, and it wasn't because they differed on the child's behavior. The mom shared how the father would take off on the weekends. When the father was at the center, there was no real father-son contact. Most children would say, "That's my daddy," or "Daddy, I love you." During a conversation with him, I learned he majored in health studies. I even tried to get him to come in and do a male involvement workshop with the fathers only. He just didn't connect, or I failed to meet him in a comfort place where he would be okay; instead, willfully or unwittingly, he prevented his son from getting the assessment he desperately needed.

This particular type of assessment would identify underlying issues, what made him laugh and cry uncontrollably, and how he could have been helped. What bothered me was how this child was dismissed simply because the father waited until the day before the assessment and said, "I don't want them assessing my child." Despite the fact the mother, the custodial parent, signed, dated, and completed the paperwork for this assessment, when the father said "no," the agency responsible stated, "His name is on the birth certificate, he's the dad, he has rights, so we have to respect his wishes." My question was, what about the mother? Her name is on the birth certificate too; doesn't that mean anything? She's the custodial parent, and if she agreed and signed for her child to get the assessment, this child's needs should have been met, not about the father's pride. This little boy had a serious issue that stood in the way of his social/emotional health, and he needed help at age four and a half, not to grow up in a world of tears, running around uncontrollably.

Throughout my teaching career, I find that whether I'm in San Francisco, Oakland, or Brooklyn, New York, there are, and will be, children with difficulties, whether mental, physical, behavioral, or neurological. They are everywhere. And parents who either are in denial or just have a hard time accepting that their child is not the perfect child they perceive is not a reason to refuse to help their child. I have to learn and accept that because I'm in a certain city or simply because I'm me, it doesn't mean parents, fellow teachers, or administrators will openly and receptively accept what I say. It's a big challenge working with children with speech defects, who are unable to focus, have a short attention span, especially children as young as two years old, because many are forming language development, or their first language may not be English.

Young children, especially in school settings, are becoming familiar with social and interaction skills, and it may not be easy, especially if they are an only child or the youngest; their home environment plays a part in how they interact. Several years ago, when I was working in Bushwick, I had a two-year-old little girl who was very aggressive with the boys in class. It was before breakfast during drop-off; these two little boys were sitting in the library looking at books. The little girl was sitting across from them, then suddenly, she lashed out at them. I quickly intervened, asking her if everything was alright, and gave the boys a hug, asking them if they were okay. I sat with her with a book to deter her attention away from them. When I spoke with her mom, it turned out she has a brother seven years older than her who fights her. I did ask the mom how she felt about that. More importantly, the assistant teacher and I, with ideas from our center director, were able to work and help the little girl manage her aggression. We also maintained positive contact with the mom. It's very important to have the assistance of the center director when working with young children who display disruptive, challenging behavior during interactions with other children, such as pushing, shoving, hitting, or attempting to bite, especially when these actions are unprovoked. This is why it's vital and lifesaving to tackle aggressive behavior and developmental delays when children are as young as eighteen months old. Therefore, it's important to have a center team of caring staff, including mental health providers, teachers, center directors, education coordinators, and disability/special-needs coordinators, working and assisting parents in the process to understand that help and support for the parent/family, as well as the child, is available.

Parents must understand that pushing, shoving, biting, scratching, anger, yelling, cursing, suffering with long crying spells, hitting, kicking, punching, and slapping their friends and teachers are not and never acceptable social behaviors. They also need to understand that their children suffer from isolation because other children are afraid of them and/or push them away due to their aggressive, violent behavior. Children who have no speech or sound, have crying spells or cry for no reason, flap their hands, or bang their hands or heads on a hard surface, such as tables or sand/water tables, could have a possible neurological delay that would require their child's pediatrician.

I had a little boy in my class at Clarkson and Rogers like that. He could be so sweet and had the cutest smile, but at two and a half years old, he had a filthy mouth, and sometimes it wasn't until lunchtime before he composed himself. Even then, we still did what we had to do. We sat with him in circle time as my teacher assistant held him; we still included him in activities, and at playtime, the ball was thrown at him, or we took him by the hand and ran him around the gym. If these toddlers do this at school, you know they must be doing this at home. What I have described is what myself and other early childhood educators nationwide deal with daily. As for this little boy, a therapist working with another child in my class witnessed and was concerned about this child's behavior. She spoke with the mother, and I continued to speak with the mom. The parents consented to his evaluation.

One challenge I had was my lack of communication with one little boy's grandmother. The child was dropped off with a soiled diaper. So instead of talking with my director and her about handling this situation, I let my attitude kick in, which led us to become cold toward one another. We would speak, but it was very dry: "Hi, how are you today? Have a good day." As a Black woman and grandmother, I should have been more supportive of not only the little boy but also her. I could see and hear what she had to deal with. I can relate that every family wants their children to be 100 percent normal. As "seasoned" Black women, we can see and hear without a word coming out of our mouths. But I was the one who behaved unprofessionally. I should have stuck by my golden rule, "a sister helping another," especially since I was on both sides of the fence and worked as a residential counselor for seven years. I became judgmental instead of being supportive and understanding that she was a grandmother having to raise a young child. I will never let that opportunity pass me by anymore because, at the end of each day, I have to take responsibility because I am the lead teacher, a seasoned woman, a mother and grandmother, a Black woman who overcame addiction, depression, and a dysfunctional lifestyle. Therefore, taking care of every child is my responsibility, from toileting to mealtime to activity time to sleep time. This includes building a trustworthy relationship with each and every parent/caregiver, assisting them with referrals, conducting follow-ups, weekly phone and in-person check-ins, and conducting classroom events, bringing our parents. "Train up a child" (Proverbs 22:6).

I share these experiences for two reasons: first, as parents, we have an obligation in rearing our children. That includes helping them in need, teaching right from wrong, how to be kind, respectful, and helpful to others. Providing spiritual teachings through age-appropriate literature, taking them weekly to church service, mosque, or temple. Ensuring they get the best education, helping them with their homework, meeting and working with their teachers. Getting your child involved in after-school and Saturday activities helps to build their character, develop their social skills and academic, creative, and physical development. They learn teamwork and how to be a team player. "Train up a child" (Proverbs 22:6). "All thy children shall be taught of the Lord" (Isaiah 54:13). "And ye fathers, provoke not your children to wrath" (Ephesians 6:4). Not only do these scriptures reinforce our parenting, but they also reinforce our relationship with God. So when troubled times come dealing with our children, be it at school, at home, or in the neighborhood, we can call on our God to help us through our crisis.

While at the site on Clarkson and Rogers, my coteacher Ms. T was very artistic and creative. She was an HBCU graduate. One of her many projects was "Parent Appreciation Day." It was held on a Friday afternoon from 4:00 to 5:00 p.m. As parents, we need that tender loving care, and having the classroom/center staff show this appreciation helps to build a stronger relationship in developing children. At TEC, my coteacher Ms. C knew several of the parents in our class; she was the art and communications specialist in the class. She, too, was working on her BA and obtaining her assistant teacher credential. Both women were qualified as lead teachers because they were in the position of lead teachers. Their actions, skills, and creativity brought uniqueness to the classroom in creating a parent-friendly environment. "In all things shewing thyself a pattern of good works: in doctrine shewing uncorruptness, gravity, sincerity, Sound speech, that cannot be condemned; that he that is of the contrary part may be ashamed, having no evil thing to say of you" (Titus 2:7–8 KJV).

Throughout my career in teaching, family advocacy, and residential counseling, I've learned to work in a setting of teamwork with different staff members to assist our children and families. But in the last two years, I'm working on the fact that teaching is my job. There should be no room inside me for grudges against parents. When I'm in a grudge mood or judgmental mood, I can't focus on what's important: helping a child grow to his/her potential and developing a lifelong relationship. As a teacher, advocate, and counselor, I've seen some of my families/clients outside the job, and I don't want those encounters to be filled with anger and resentment. I want our encounters to continue to be friendly and positive. When I'm judgmental, resentful, and unprofessional, parents/caregivers have a right to be concerned about their child in my care. They want to know if I'm that way with them, then how am I treating their child?

In closing, as my daddy would tell me as a child and teenager, "Victoria, it's easier to catch bees with honey than with vinegar." In other words, treat people the way I want to be treated. "But to do good and to communicate forget not: for with such sacrifices God is well pleased" (Hebrews 13:16 KJV).

I'm More than Disgruntled

One of my worst experiences as an ECE student was in June 2019. I wanted to transfer from City College of New York to Brooklyn College, which is much closer to where I live. I scheduled an appointment by email and was contacted by the college's ECE department for an interview to get into the ECE master's program. Since attending and passing my ECE course at CCNY-CUNY in the fall of 2018, I thought the transition to the ECE program at Brooklyn College would be easy. First off, I assumed that since CCNY and Brooklyn colleges are under the CUNY (City University of New York) system, they would have the same agenda for the ECE master's program. I was sorely wrong.

The disappointment began the moment I walked into the door at the college's ECE department. My appointment was scheduled for 12:30 p.m., to meet with the assistant department chair. I left work at 11:30 a.m., and when I got there, the department's administrative assistant wasn't very receptive. I asked if I should sit in the office, and she was like, "You can sit in the hallway," which I did. By 1:00 p.m., I was thinking to myself, "What's taking this woman so long?" By 1:15 p.m., I went into the office to ask the secretary about Professor S. She spoke in a stern tone, "She's coming. You just have to wait." There was no consideration for my time or the fact that I left my job to come there for an interview where the interviewer was not on-site. I actually saw the department chair, Dr. S., and she never said a word or came out of her office or had the courtesy to say, "Can I help you?" There was no picking up the slack for the professor who was not on-site. Around 1:30 p.m., I asked again about Professor S., and that's when I was told that she was on the train and there was a delay due to the weather. A train delay, bad weather, really? It was a light rain, not a storm.

Around 1:45 p.m., the associate professor finally arrived. Within five minutes, she called me into her office, offering no apology, nor did she say, "I'm sorry you had to wait so long." I felt like the associate professor conducted herself unprofessionally and in a noncaring manner about my time.

I used my lunch break and planned on getting back to the center before the children awoke from their nap. As we spoke about the possibility of getting accepted into the ECE master's program, she started focusing on my 2.39 GPA from San Francisco State University. In order to get into the ECE master's program, I would have to have a 2.50. I presented to her my recent CUNY-CCNY official transcript. I pointed out I got an A with a GPA of 3.0. You would think with the recent CUNY transcript that would get me into the ECE program. I asked about coming in as a nonmatriculation student. Her focus was on my SFSU unofficial transcript with a 2.39 GPA. Again, I asked, "What about my transcript from CCNY?" The professor would not answer my question. By then, the department head joined in. She told me I would have to take several certification exams as a requirement of getting into the master's program. I asked her if there was a certification preparation class. She did not answer. I had to ask three times about the class prep course. At that point, Dr. S. appeared agitated and then stated the program didn't have funding for that. I said I could go ahead and take an ECE course in the fall, but Dr. S stated, "You need to focus on the certifications." Then I was told I would not be accepted into the master's ECE program. I asked if I would receive an email verifying this, and I was told yes by Dr. S. Professor S didn't say anything; she just stood there. I also mentioned the $75 application fee I paid and wanted to know if I would get that back. Neither could answer that question. As for receiving an email of denial for the ECE program at Brooklyn College for fall 2019, I never received any type of correspondence of my denial into the ECE master's program. After meeting with these two women, they referred me to meet with a woman in certification, and she was no help either. She gave me a form where I would have to do classroom fieldwork, then she wrote down information about certification exams.

I left feeling angry because I felt like my time was wasted and I felt disrespected. I mean, the State and Department of Education say we have to go to school until we get our BA or MA and pass three certifications, yet they make the curriculum complicated. I have an associate of arts degree in child development, a bachelor's degree in liberal studies, a combined ten years of classroom experience, six and a half years of experience as a Head Start Family Advocate, and seven years of experience as a residential counselor, and I'm an ECE lead teacher working with two- to three-year-olds. Yet I can't get into a master's program? There's no adviser I could connect with that would even mentor me.

Around January 2020, I received an email and phone call from the college's ECE program to come and complete my ECE application. I'm not putting myself through this again. I completed my application, paid my seventy-five-dollar nonrefundable fee, showed up on time for the June 18, 2019, interview only to be inconvenienced by having to wait on the interviewer for an hour and a half, with no apology, only to be denied entry into the Brooklyn College ECE master's program, which I never received a formal email or letter stating my denial. At that time, I was already employed and I completed the fall semester at CUNY-CCNY.

The fact that I didn't get accepted into the program because of my GPA of 2.39 from San Francisco State University, which was dumb since I graduated in May 2004, then attended CUNY-CCNY in the fall of 2018 in which I got an A with a GPA of 3.7, along with my résumé of experience with children and families, wasn't even considered. Getting accepted into the ECE master's program would've been great since it's right here in Brooklyn and not far from where

I live. Thank God I was still enrolled at City College of New York in the fall of 2019. I took two classes: I got a B in an ECE course and a C in math, so my GPA dropped. I also contacted Dr. B at CCNY's ECE master's program in early 2020; she informed me since my GPA dropped below a B average, I couldn't get into the program and she had no advice or assistance for me. I was like, never mind the fact that my work history as a child development teacher, residential counselor, and family advocate experience spoke for me. What else I had to realize: I could be angry at this experience, but it was also a learning experience for me. I had to make a rational decision not to let what has happened be the reason for me not to move forward with my education.

Moving forward to the fall of 2020, I enrolled in an ECE Zoom class at Touro College and got an A. In January 2021, I enrolled in my second Zoom course through Touro College, and in April, I had a left-knee replacement, which left me out of work on disability, but I was able to complete my class and pass with flying colors. With my state disability and retirement being only half of my employment pay, by September 2021, I started preparing to return to work, reregistered with Workforce 1, along with interview, résumé, and cover letter workshops. Then I did a Zoom "career advice" session with my career adviser. I applied for positions and interviewed for Family Advocate and Head Start Home Visitor. My education goal was to attend Brooklyn College in the spring of 2022 and continue to seek a degree in education to meet the New York State DOE guidelines.

By October 2021, I had to pump the brakes after going back to my teaching jobsite. The site director concluded that because of my knee replacement, I could not physically meet the classroom standards for two- to three-year-olds. She even told me if there were an emergency that would require me to pick up the kids: again, let me point out there are eight toddlers and two teachers, and several of those two- to three-year-olds weighed twenty-five to thirty pounds. First off, if there were an emergency that warranted me to pick up the children, I could only pick up one child at a time, and second, the other teacher could only pick up one child, so who's going to pick up the other six children? Within several days, the executive director and I had a conversation, and she informed me that I would not be rehired, then she quickly stated she wouldn't contest me applying for state unemployment. I applied for unemployment and started searching for jobs. I decided to look for family advocates; to heck with classroom teaching—I'm done. Also, since the holiday seasons were approaching, I applied for a Christmas job at Macy's, got selected, did the orientation, and once the background check cleared, I officially started work at Macy's Thirty-Fourth Street in the Santaland department as a cashier on November 30, 2021.

Now that I'm working Christmas part-time at Macy's, I called Touro College's finance department to work out a payment plan for my fall 2021 tuition. To my surprise, funding was given to help students like me who didn't qualify for financial aid and/or couldn't even get a scholarship. The woman in finance told me that President Biden gave the school money and my debt was paid. She said to me, "Merry Christmas." Then, on Friday, December 17, I received a call from Cardinal McCloskey Community Service with a family-advocate job offer. What a great Christmas holiday season for me. Now, I'm looking at attending school in fall 2022, along with changing my major to theater and arts with a minor in literature. Currently, I'm studying piano. I've already written a play, I'm writing sermons, my knee chronicle journal, and I'm working on this book. God is good, and it's time I get rid of my attitude and get with and continue with the plan and program He has for me.

Can I get some help? AKA Quality Childcare

The Lord shall fight for you, and ye shall
hold your peace.

—Exodus 14:14 KJV

As I sit here thinking about the foundation of humanity in the
areas of social-emotional, cognitive thinking, problem-solving, along
with science, math, literacy, art, large gross motor skills/athletics,
physical health, nutrition, and mental health. Teaching our children
how to value their health, dental hygiene, and what is being put into
their spiritual, physical, and mental being of each child is the real
foundation of humanity.

Education in the United States of America today has always
been based on skin color, neighborhood, zip code, and economic
status. My family lived in the Hunter's Point project located in the
southeast section of San Francisco. Some of the schools in the neighborhood were inferior. The schools didn't have the best teachers, the
books were used, the average kid in Hunter's Point was at least a
grade to two to three grades behind academically. When I started
attending public school in the sixth grade at Hunter's Point 2 (no
longer in existence), half of my classmates were reading and doing
math at a third-grade level. I made the mistake by saying to several
classmates they couldn't read. I got chased home from school. My
sisters and I were fortunate because our mother sent us to Catholic

school for two reasons: we were Catholic and she wanted us to get a good Christian education. In our home, we had books of every kind and on every subject from children to science to history to literature.

In 1972, Momma ordered a complete set of *Britannica Encyclopedia*; it came with a set of junior and children's encyclopedias. You could say we had a mini-library of our own. Momma would always stress to us the importance of reading and education. She would put her hand up and, using each finger, say, "You should always ask the five *W*'s: who, what, where, when, and why." When I was, like, nine and ten years old, I would be ready to go outside and play with my friends; Momma would pump my brakes and tell me to read a book. I'm trying to go outside, and she wants me to take time to read! Really? I just wanted to die. Imagine that, my own mother denying me the right to play, all because she wants me to educate my mind. Oh, let me add, my father supported this weird theory. My parents (no longer with us), I still say thank you, Momma and Daddy. Because of them, I get my creativity in writing, reading, as well as music.

Pops was like a living history book. As far as I know, he never graduated from high school. It was his life's experience, growing up in Jim Crow St. Louis, Missouri, and by his widowed mother, making a decision to fight in a war for a country that refused to see him as a man, in World War II, and his adventures while in Europe. His favorite place in the world was Rome, Italy. He told us about the paintings of Michelangelo and going to the Vatican. My father fought in France, Germany, and North Africa. Whenever we had homework assignments, especially Black history assignments, he shared firsthand accounts of Jim Crow, what it was like for him to serve his country and have to deal with racism on the battlefields of Europe and here in the United States. Despite Momma and Daddy growing up in a society where racism was so blatant, they taught us to treat people kindly. We were not allowed to criticize or judge people by the color of their skin, the sound of their last name, or where they came from. Our parents taught us that people of all races, nationalities, and cultures deserved to be respected and, before we criticize, we should get to know the person. I'm proud to say my parents were proud of who they were, and they taught us the same thing. They were also involved in community activism. They didn't mind living in the projects; what was important to them was better and equal opportunities for themselves as well as for us.

I share this because, as a teacher, it's important that we incorporate the traditions from our life experience and upbringing, which also is what many of the families we serve have in common. Along with our experience and support from our site administrators, we can be of assistance when we have challenging children, which today is all too common. Part of working with my two-year-olds included children who were diagnosed and receiving services and children who showed signs of needing services. It's about observation, noticing a pattern. It's not always what they're doing but what they're not doing. In 2018, I had a two-year-old boy who didn't talk, but what became noticeable was that he didn't make any type of sound or laugh out loud. He would smile. His maternal grandmother was his main provider, but once in a while, his mother would drop him off at school and sit in the classroom for up to an hour. Because of my personal experience, I could tell she was not the main caregiver of her child, and I noticed there was no real mother-son interaction. The little boy didn't sit next to his mom or even hug her the way he hugged his grandmother. I'm not going to spend a lot of time analyzing this family, but I will say I could've done more on my part as the child's teacher to bridge the gap between me and the grandmother. I do hold her accountable because she would bring that child to school with a soiled diaper filled with urine and poop. Upon our school closure on June 28, 2019, the center's family worker assisted this family in getting this child into a sister site, which was good because this child needed interaction with other children and whatever assistance that could benefit him.

In October 2021, while I was still on disability (left-knee replacement), I visited the center I worked at in Bushwick on Broadway Street. As I pressed my way to all the classrooms, saying hi to the office staff, the director, coworkers, and children, in the pre-K classroom, this one little girl who recently returned was literally trying to run out of the classroom with one teacher staying with her while the other teacher had to monitor the other children. The center director came in, so I was able to give a history of this little girl. She was in the two- to three-year-old classroom next door. She was nonverbal then and nonresponsive when her name was called. From my understanding, the family dropped her from the program when this child could've started getting help at age two; in 2021, at four years old, with no progress, she was yelling, still nonverbal, and fighting to run out of the classroom. The reality is, in my professional opinion, this child needed to be in a special-education environment where she would get more attention and her needs would be met along with several therapists and a classroom ratio of at least three teachers to nine children at the most.

It is challenging, painful, and even angering for parents/caregivers to face the reality that their child is not like the other children. Their child is not running, laughing, nonresponsive when their name is called or when talking to the child; they're not talking (they cry and/or make sounds at three, four, or five years old); they're not able to run, jump, or even hold a pencil or eating utensil; they don't interact with other children and teachers. What's challenging for the classroom teacher is the resistance from parents/caregivers and lack of support from center administrators, support staff, and mental health specialists. I had one mental health specialist who was on-site one day a week, and she spent her time observing the teachers' interaction with children, then she'd leave the classroom and come back with a list of one hundred things to do in the classroom. We're asking the mental health specialist to observe certain children, their behavior, and their interaction/reaction with other children and the teachers, and this professional is checking out what the teachers are doing. And to think, she had a master's degree.

Note: I know personally, as a family member, what it's like to have a child who needs help coping with basic life skills or a child diagnosed with autism, ADHD, and born with a genetic illness. The child in our family with the genetic illness passed away at three and a half. I also know what it's like to have more than one child, with my two oldest daughters eleven months apart. I can relate to a lot of parents, especially single Black mothers, and what they experience. This is what helps me as a teacher, along with my Christian teachings. I can speak wisdom and, at the same time, keep the relationship open with the parents/caregivers.

Children displaying developmental delays, behavior issues, nonverbal communication, screaming, yelling, cursing, and fighting at school are also doing it at home. Sticking your head in the sand and leaving it solely to the child's teacher is not going to solve the problem. It's just like parents/caregivers whose three-year-old still drinks from baby bottles or sippy cups, still wearing diapers, yet they expect the child's teacher to magically do the work. In October 2020, during a weekly phone contact with a parent, the discussion was around toileting her child. In a rude tone, she told me, "You need to take initiative," in toilet training her child. At that point, I forcefully told this woman thank you and hung up the phone. I told my coteacher what she said; her response was, "Really?" As for me, being a Christian woman, a seasoned woman, and not wanting to lose my job helped me to contain the choice words for this mother. Not to mention, this was a parent who had no control over her child, as I witnessed myself during the parent-teacher conference. Since it was early pickup, the mother surprisingly gave up twenty minutes for the parent-teacher conference. The child sat next to her mom at a child-sized table and chair with blocks, paper, and crayons. This child attempted to climb over the table, ran around the classroom, and when the mother asked her to come sit down, this child looked straight into her mother's eyes and said, "No," as if "You don't tell me what to do." My c-teacher and I continued our end to assist the child as well as the other seven children in toileting. At one point, she was progressing, then she started regressing by her third birthday; that's when we found out her mother was pregnant. The parents of this little girl were not willing to receive suggestions; they didn't even bother to ask how their child's day went. They were like some other parents I've encountered in my years of teaching who actually have said, "You're the teacher," "It's your job," "You figure it out." On a spiritual level, since the parent is the child's first teacher, the child's first encounter, therefore, the parents have the responsibility to do all they can to help their child. "The rod and reproof give wisdom: but a child left to himself bringeth his mother to shame" (Proverbs 29:15 KJV). "Train up a child in the way he should go: and when he is old, he will not depart from it" (Proverbs 22:6 KJV). "Fathers, provoke not your children to anger, lest they be discouraged" (Colossians 3:21 KJV). There are other Bible scriptures that support parenting and children who are commanded to honor thy mother and thy father. In closing, if a man is married to a woman and he fathers a child outside his marriage, he is held accountable and liable to assist in raising this child, financially and mentally supporting this child. It's his problem to deal with his wife since he violated his wedding vows. The same for the mother if she's married and gets pregnant by another man. Teachers, center directors, family court judges, family court attorneys, school principals, school social workers, mental health specialists, child protective social workers, youth ministers, pastors, bishops, school nurses, residential counselors, probation officers, and all others who directly work with children/families have the responsibility to assist, help children and families meet their needs, not to play favorites, hold over a parent's head, "I got your child, I can do what I want." If possible, reunify families. Help these children, bring out the best in them so that they will grow to be independent and be the best they can be.

Closing out this chapter, let's take another final look at what I perceive quality childcare to be and the most important foundations in our children, families, and communities. It's important spiritually, mentally, academically, creatively, and socially. Without quality childcare, there is no real growth. You grow, but there's always something that's not there.

Quality childcare focuses on increasing a child's mental intellect, socialization with their peers, their teachers, and their peer's family members. Quality childcare focuses on monthly community/parent meetings and workshops centered on parenting, health and nutrition, parent involvement, literacy/education, and mental health services/support. Quality childcare supports classroom teachers by providing three teachers instead of two per classroom and providing teachers with financial assistance in tuition and books to further their education in areas needed most, which is special education.

Quality childcare

- introduces children to celebrate their roots through dance, songs, story time, and crafts;
- provides health, dental, and good nutritional services;
- includes parents, supporting them with family assessments, two home visits per school year, and individualized parent goal plans;
- teaches children to identify with who they are, not just their culture;
- offers parents monthly workshops in child development, child literacy, health/nutrition, importance of immunizations, dental hygiene, asthma information, domestic violence, financial education, voter registration, and community activism, among other topics;
- recruits parent volunteers, as per the regulations of the office of Head Start;
- encompasses quality education, where grown adults with families of their own still fondly recall their school experiences. I still share mine about growing up in All Hallows School and church, where we were a family.

We pour ourselves into the families we serve, alongside dealing with our own personal issues such as death in our families, sickness, incarceration, separation, divorce, abandonment, financial difficulties, and even domestic violence. This can create divisions because, as teachers, we may begin to see ourselves or our own family members in the families we serve, which can lead to dislike, distrust, and burnout. When we take the time to be a part of quality childcare through self and job care, quality childcare becomes effective, leaving everyone, primarily the children, in a win-win situation.

A Goal-Setting Thought

Trust in the Lord with all thine heart; and lean not unto thine own understanding. In all thy ways acknowledge Him, and He shall direct thy paths.

—Proverbs 3:5–6 KJV

A goal-setting thought—now, that is something. But as a kid, teenager, young adult, and until I got clean, I wasn't aware of goals, let alone a goal-setting thought. As a kid, I was a dreamer, and a big one at that. I'd dream about having an upstairs-downstairs house. I dreamed about becoming a movie star or a soul and blues singer. Then, as a teenager, going with my friends to see Black movies or television shows filmed in or about New York City / Harlem, I thought, *That's it, I'm moving to Harlem where I would be around nothing but Black people, going to the Apollo...* But I didn't really think much about anything else I'd do once I would (dream) move to Harlem.

Once I got pregnant while still in high school, many dream possibilities went out the window; they became far and very few. By 1979, I was no longer dreaming; I just lived in the present. Whatever happened, I went with the flow, whether it was a party at the end of the workweek or staying up all night smoking weed laced with cocaine. If there was a dream floating around in my head, I wouldn't have known it; my head was clouded, and I lived outside myself.

By 1985, with four children, I would often imagine what it would be like if Bill and I were married. I imagined us having a home, working, and taking care of our children. Then I'd snap back to reality: I was living with my mother with four children. There was nothing wrong with that; what was wrong was my drug habit, my temper, and my frustration with who I was, which was continuously escalating.

"Set your affection on things above, not on things on the earth" (Colossians 3:2 KJV).

It wasn't until the last part of my addiction, beginning in early 1994, that I started thinking about my children. How I wanted to be a mother again. It became a determination, but it was just "How?" How was I going to restore my life? I took some steps, such as minimizing my crack and hard-alcohol usage, especially the first few days after receiving my GA check on the first and fifteenth. I would smoke weed and drink beer. I would get jobs that didn't last more than a month or two. I had the desire to want to change, but I couldn't because I always ended up with the "pipe in my mouth."

"If then I do that which I would not, I consent unto the law that it is good. Now then it is no more I that do it, but sin that dwelleth in me. For I know that in me (that is, in my flesh) dwelleth no good thing: for to will is present with me; but how to perform that which is good I find not" (Romans 7:16–18 KJV).

To fast-forward to July 13, 1994, to December 4, 1994, I don't recall the words "goal" and "goal setting." What I do recall was working on myself: making sure I showed up every day for twenty weeks to my outpatient program, going to therapy, attending women's meetings, talking about my problems and issues that nearly led me to total self-destruction, going to meetings (NA and AA), learning and working the 12 steps, staying clean, and most of all, staying away from shaky people, places, and things that could lead me back to active addiction. I'm doing what I desire to do, what I've always wanted to do; I just didn't realize or equate this to goal setting. I didn't see completing my twenty-week outpatient program as a goal; I saw it as "Finally, for once in my life, I completed something." I saw that I could succeed. The next step was to get out of the shelter, get my own place to live, and then get a job.

I was introduced to goal setting when I returned to City College of San Francisco in the fall of 1995 by my EOPS counselor. The first thing was, I had to deal with the fact I would be on probation academically as well as financially, meaning I had to take several courses over again, maintaining good attendance, and pass with at least a C or better. Although I applied for financial aid with work-study, I couldn't get it until the spring of 1996. I got it—no, I don't. I would set goals, but I didn't know I was setting goals. Working as a residential counselor from 2000 to 2007 and working as a Head Start family advocate, I did become more familiarized with the term "goal setting"; I just didn't apply it to myself. The goal-setting thought didn't hit me until 2018 after I moved to Brooklyn and started back working as a childcare teacher. My site directors would ask me, "Victoria, what are your goals?" "What do you want to do?" "What are the steps you will need to take to reach your goal?"

Today, it's a goal-setting thought that keeps me motivated. I look forward to living life each day because I have goals. As I prepare to retire, a goal I'm working on is to be debt-free. Recently, I paid off my personal loan with a monthly payment of $271.11. For me, that's a large debt to pay monthly, and paying this off has lifted a weight off me. Reapplying for college, actually starting class in spring 2024, getting my own apartment, getting my website in order to promote my book sales as well as my skincare and beauty consulting business are among my goals. I'm working on a goal now: completing my bio and revising *Who Am, I Am*, then submitting both manuscripts to the publisher. Part of the goal is editing both manuscripts, then presenting them to three people to read and ask for reviews. Once completed, the manuscripts will be forwarded to the publisher. I get excited thinking about this because I'm not letting my age hold me back. In conclusion, trusting in God when my back is against the wall, my goals and sanity are at stake, what do I do? I take a breather, pray, and know that God is in charge, and he has my back always. "Delight thyself also in the Lord, and do good; and He shall give thee the desires of thine heart. Commit thy way unto the Lord; trust also unto Him; and He shall bring it to pass" (Psalm 37:4–5 KJV).

Who Am, I Am published in 2020

Victoria Stith and God's Anointed Children: CD release 2014

The CD was completed in 2014: Monica was living in
Texas during the making of the CD. Damarr Jr drummer,
Kaia vocalist, John-Paul aka JP keyboard/vocalist

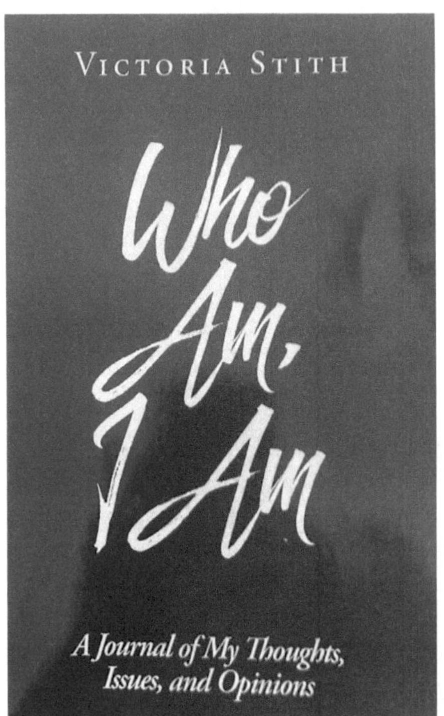

Who am, I am was released in early 2020 at
the beginning of the pandemic.

Section 4

✦

Trusting in God

When in doubt, trust God.
When not sure, trust God.

Take responsibility for my actions and my mistakes. Trust God.
Don't use other family members, friends, and anyone to take myself away from myself. Instead trust God.

"Behold, God is my salvation; I will trust, and not be afraid: for the Lord JEHOVAH is my strength and my song; he also is become my salvation" (Isaiah 12:2 KJV).

Failure 2 Success

And be not conformed to this world; be ye transformed by the renewing of your mind, that ye may prove what that is good, and acceptable, and perfect, will of God.

—Romans 12:2 KJV

When I look back, choosing to fail was not the fault of others; it was my fault. I can see now that I internalized my problems, and some problems I didn't have to go through. But for me, I looked outside at what others had and then wondered why that couldn't be me. Why couldn't I just accept the fact that when my mother enrolled me in a private school? To be honest, I don't recall if she told me she was going. It was my chance to live a good life; here I was, this Black girl from Hunter's Point, going to this school where people were different. The class sizes were small; I mean, like, maybe ten at the most per class. There was no class cutting, no smoking cigarettes in the girls' bathroom, none of that stuff. Yet I found it difficult to adjust to this nice, clean environment, despite that in all honesty, I liked the school and I did make friends. In fact, one of the friends I made, we reconnected on social media two years ago. The failure in that was I ended up back in Pelton doing the same thing my mother wanted to remove me from.

When I fast-forward to Sunday, July 10, 1994, I saw that "Okay, Vickie, you made this promise to God, now stick with it." For the first time in my entire thirty-seven and a half years at that time, I was going to do something and I wasn't going to mess this up. Starting with that weekend, everything intertwined itself—you know, it's like hemming your pants. The end result: they look great; in fact, they almost look new, and that's how I felt. So immediately, I sought refuge because in order to succeed, I had to go where I knew I would be supported, to Glide and then to the shelter for safety off the streets, a good meal, and a warm bed. Getting up in the morning wasn't a problem for me because I had somewhere to go; that place was Glide. The first three days of my sobriety, I did hustle my cans, plastic, and glass, but I left it alone for two reasons: first off, I was on GA (general assistance for single people) and food stamps. The second reason was, the hustling was how I survived in the streets; it was how I got my first high of the day, going by selling cans, glass, and plastic. For years, I left recycling alone because at that time, continuing could've led me back to using. Isn't God amazing? He put the spirit of success in me, and I didn't even know or realize it. (Just a quick note: I did, after my ten-year mark in recovery, pick up recycling due to extra cash and to assist in fundraising for our family gospel business, Vicstar Productions.)

Due to my commitment that I would never leave Hunter's Point until the day I died, when I got clean, God got to work on me right away. I was accustomed to the perimeter of Hunter's Point, Fillmore, and Tenderloin in San Francisco, Forty-Seventh and West Streets in North Oakland, and Eighty-Second Avenue in East Oakland; that kept me locked away from the rest of the world. As long as I lived in that space, I was a sure failure because this world is where I used, drank, and lived a homeless, pathetic life. Once I made my pact with God that if he helped me, I would never get high again, the road for me to succeed opened up. One of the requirements while in day treatment was to attend a meeting a day (at least seven meetings per week). For some, it may seem like a lot, but to a person like me who was and still is serious about recovery, it's not asking a whole lot. I got an AA and NA meeting schedule, having to fit in the meetings into my time schedule. I attended a meeting in the Marina District in the northwestern part of San Francisco; in fact, if you drive down Lombard Street, it takes you to the Golden Gate Bridge. Attending the program daily, support groups such as women's group, group and individual therapy, 12-step groups, and any other type of support group and workshop that would help was another failure to success for me. In 1994, I didn't see it as "failure to success"; what I did see was keeping my promise not to get high, and if my counselors told me to stand on one foot and pat the top of my head daily for ten minutes in order to stay clean, I would've done so.

This whole concept of why I named this chapter "Failure 2 Success" is because of God's phenomenal works on and for me. It flowed; there was no waiting period where, "Okay, Vickie, I hear you. I'll help you, but you have to wait." The very people at the program who helped me were once drug users, convicts, and dysfunctional themselves. He turned their lives around so they can be blessings, counselors, administrators, and mentors to people like me. By July 1994, it was my third time trying to stay clean, and this time I succeeded. For me to be in the circle Monday through Friday and get chopped up, peeled like a banana, and then come back the next day, I had to be crazy or really serious. They genuinely cared about me; they didn't laugh at me. Instead, there were even different ways for me to let go or share about my life experiences. There were women's groups; there was the individual therapy. I slowly went from "No, I can't" to "Oh yes, I will." I was determined to do this; I promised God, and I was not going back on my word with him. He was my only and last hope.

The road to success didn't come easy; I had to work at it. And I didn't change overnight, and I didn't change by the end of the program in December 1994. It's a process: going to meetings, minding my own business, facing my flaws, dealing with how I fell into drug and alcohol addiction. What I did to my family, my community, and most of all, myself. I had to deal with my relationship with Bill or showing up in the group with my soda in a bag like it was a can of beer. Breaking me from the bad habit of carrying two plastic bags of paper: documents I considered important, along with undergarments and toiletries. I had to change every aspect of my life: how I thought, how I talked, what streets I walked down. I had to change friends; no longer did I hang with street associates but with people who lived and stayed clean and sober. I had to change the fact that I was worth something. I was worth fighting for. I didn't know what I was getting into, but as I said earlier, I made a promise to God, and I was sticking to it.

Eighteen months into my recovery, I had to make the move I didn't want to make; that was getting a sponsor. I attended a weekly step study meeting because misunderstanding shares at the meetings, I thought that working that fourth step would cause me to relapse, so I avoided getting a sponsor. I don't know what I expected from a sponsor, but I picked a sponsor who was honest; she did not hold back on the truth, and she cared about me.

I'll never forget I finally started working on step four. My sponsor says to me to make two lists: what I did to others and what others did to me. She was like, "Put your name on the top of both columns." I asked her, "Why would I put my name on the list?" She looked at me and said, "You don't think you did damage to yourself?" As I began writing, the list was longer than I expected. I found that everyone in my life, from my parents, to my sisters, my children, neighbors, friends, church members, and others, I did something to. But when it came to what I did to myself, that was a long list as well. I had to apologize to these people; she suggested I write "Dear God" letters, especially to those who were deceased like my father and grandmother Mary or those whom I did wrong to but who didn't realize I wronged them. We had a family friend who knew me since my teen years. During the height of my getting high, I got high with him several times. His wife, his family, as well as my mother would've been furious with me that I got high with him. If my father were alive at that time, he would've been angry and hurt at me and him because this was my father's friend as well. The fact that his friend was smoking crack with his daughter. I couldn't walk up to her, the family, or even my mother and say, "I'm sorry I got high with [name]"; this is where the "Dear God" letters come in. I start the letter: "Dear God, [in parentheses put the person's name], I'm sorry I did…" Processing and writing the "Dear God" letter to Grandma Mary, I felt like I let her down when I got pregnant at eighteen when, in actuality, she got sick and died two weeks before Mikey was born. For years, I carried this burden on my back. I blamed myself for her death; I felt like I broke her heart.

My EOPS counselor, the administrative assistant, and several of my instructors also contributed to my changing from a failure to becoming a success. I got involved with STAR (Students Talk About Racism), which was facilitated by then SFPD Sgt. L., whose father was a pastor in Lakeview, a.k.a. Ingleside. It was one semester for six weeks; every Tuesday, the group I was in met with ninth-grade US history students during their second period. In this group, we would mostly observe and watch the students discuss racism and stereotypes from their teenage perspective. It was very interesting watching these students process their thoughts on this subject matter. I hope that this group discussion left a positive impact on them.

While I was at CCSF, one of my child development instructors, Sue R., an older white woman, mentored me in the classes I needed. I remember taking several courses in Infant-Toddler. I said to her, "I'm not changing any diaper," but she insisted I would need these courses. I did end up taking and passing the infant-toddler courses.

While at CCSF, I met this sister; we were about the same age, which was refreshing because we could talk to each other. She told me she was in the Black Student Union, so I joined the BSU. Being in the BSU gave me the opportunity to speak at Downtown High School. This was a school where challenging students went. These students were smart; they just had a lot of problems. I was honored to be able to speak with and before them. The real success for me was my graduation from City College of San Francisco on May 13, 1997; now that was a true success story for me. This was like, "Wow," I did it; I accomplished an important life-changing goal in my life.

Also in 1997, with the help of Ms. Garcia, I got my child development permit, I got a full-time job, and, as I mentioned earlier, I had to deal with child support. In the last twenty-nine years of my life, it has been an amusement park, where I close my eyes and pick the craziest ride to get on. I've had ups and downs. I even did things on my own, but I never stopped praying, even when God stepped back and let me run my life, because when he guided me, even when I was impatient and at times ungrateful, God never left me. I never went back on my word; no matter what I went through, I stayed clean.

Today, in 2023, with twenty-nine years clean and sober, it's still important for me to ask myself how many opportunities are before me. Am I letting life pass me by? The question is, am I choosing to apply myself or not apply myself? Am I pushing myself or just giving in? Am I taking advantage by going to God in prayer? I love my son, I love my daughters, I love my grandchildren, but they have their lives to live. I can be there for them as a guide, the family matriarch, a supporter, but in the end, they have to make their own decisions. I can't live their lives or live my life through them. I need to and have to be busy living my life. I always have to ask myself, am I using them as an excuse to not push myself to be where God is directing and guiding me to be? Why have I been here so long? Do I really trust in God?

It's time for me to reach the goal by climbing the ladder God has for me. I love writing songs, books, poems, and journals. I have so much I want to say to the world. I remember in 2019 my bishop did a sermon using Abraham. Here Abram was an elderly man, up in age; his wife, Sarai, was barren, yet God kept His promise to Abram, renaming him Abraham, that his seed would be as endless as the sand on the beaches and the stars in the night sky. Sarai laughed at the fact that she would bear a child in her old age. God is a promise keeper, and believe me, God is very patient.

"But the Fruit of the Spirit is love, joy, peace, long-suffering, gentleness, meekness, faith" (Galatians 5:22 KJV).

God's plans for me have and will always be accomplished. Today, my two biggest goals are focusing on my retirement from my job by January 2024 and returning to school in January 2024. I'm glad to know that as long as I live, I trust in God and lean on the scripture, "I can do all things in Christ Jesus that strengthens me" (Philippians 4:13).

Forgive, Let Go, and Move On

For if ye forgive men their trespasses, your heavenly Father will also forgive you: But if ye forgive not men their trespasses, neither will your Father forgive your trespasses.

—Matthew 6:14–15 KJV

One of the biggest problems I had was creating my own problems, then holding on to resentments, anger, and most of all, unforgiveness. Even after I got clean, I was going to meetings, sharing, going back to church, and joining support groups like anger management, domestic violence, and codependency, yet I still held on to grudges, secret resentments, and an unwillingness to forgive people. Getting clean, getting my own place, getting a job, going to school, and going to church were great accomplishments for me, but to let go of my resentment toward those who did me wrong, I wasn't about to do that. Somehow, someway, these losers, backstabbers had to pay. Several had died, others moved on with their lives, and there were those still getting high, and they certainly weren't thinking about me. And when they did see me and saw I got myself together, the only thing they wanted from me was a couple of dollars to help get their day's supply of dope. Whew, man, learning to let go, process my past and other issues in a healthy yet sensitive way was definitely a long process.

The trauma, unforgiveness, anger, shame, guilt, embarrassment, and resentments went back to my childhood. I would just be sitting, watching a program about girls in Catholic school, then I would go back to the day I was kicked out of All Hallows School in 1968; I was in the sixth grade. I thought about that whole scenario: with me, my mom, and Sister Bridget standing in the hall outside class. Sister Bridget had that stern look. I can't remember what happened that day, but she asked me, "Do you still want to go here?" My mother went to answer, but she put her hand up to my mother, like, "Don't say anything." I started to cry, and I said, "No." Right then and there, I ended up in the classroom cleaning out my desk. I was no longer a student at All Hallows. I would spend years beating myself up. "Why did I say no?" I really missed going to All Hallows; I missed my friends.

Fast-forward to 1980, an incident I got myself into at work. This incident happened at my workplace. I was employed at Crocker National Bank (which is no longer in existence). I was pregnant with Jawana and had transferred from Primeline Credit to a department on the second floor. The manager (she was really nice) we would talk. My personal life sucked; I was pregnant with a drug habit and in a lousy relationship. It was November 1980; I cursed out a male coworker I didn't even know, and when she attempted to intervene, I cursed her out. It was one of the stupidest acts I ever committed. In February 1981, I was scheduled to return to work. When I met with the human resources specialist, she told me it was my behavior, disrespect, and insubordination toward my manager. I would've been on probation for three months, but being the weakling I was, I got mad and told the HR specialist I would rather quit the job. You can't get any more stupid and ignorant than that. I did wrong, yet I had the nerve to get bent out of shape. I should've been glad I got my job back. I had this "I don't care" attitude, along with the fact that now I'm going to be back on welfare and living with my mother. I had resentment with everyone when, in reality, I didn't want to take responsibility for my actions, let alone apologize for my horrible behavior.

In 1994, while I was in the program, it was during an afternoon group. I can't remember if I was called upon or if I opened up on my own, but I began to talk about the death of my father and the last week of his life. It started on Wednesday, January 15, 1992; I was at his house, and I owed him some money. It was check day, and I owed him something like around fifteen dollars, but I had already gotten high. He had this look like it didn't matter about the money. Then he said to me, "Vickie, why don't you spend the night? I'll go downstairs and put you on the list." Little did I know, care, or even be aware that that was the last time I saw, spoke to, or hugged my father. On Saturday, January 18, 1992, I was lying in bed asleep when a knock on the door came; I got the message my father died. "What? No, this can't be happening. It's a mistake." I waited that whole day. I just knew he would walk through the door at Momma's, and all would be well. It wasn't a mistake; it was real. Daddy was gone. But I didn't get the chance to pay him back; I didn't get to say I'm sorry. There I was, two and a half years later, in group talking about his passing, what I did to him, how I disappointed him, and most of all, how I wish he was there to see me finally, for real, get clean and sober. I stayed clean, but it took ten years to let go and accept he was gone and, most of all, to forgive myself for the wrong I did to him.

Getting a sponsor eighteen months into my recovery and working on the steps helped some in letting go of the hurt that I felt spiritually, physically, mentally, and psychologically. The trauma I endured came not only from others but mostly from myself and was of my own doing. Mental, physical, and sexual trauma, especially the sexual trauma, could've been avoided. Putting myself into harm's way—there were times I didn't listen to my mother, getting high alone with guys I would not have normally hung out with—fed into my development of resentments. The least little thing a person said and did to me, I took personally. I held on to it, even smiling in the person's face. Aside from lying to my family and friends, I lied to myself, and that is insane, because lying to myself kept me bound. That's why I stayed in the hole of addiction and was unable to get out, because I wanted others to see it my way. I believed what I wanted to believe, doing it my way, unable to accept constructive criticism, disrespect toward my parents and other adults and superiors on my jobs, not listening, and being disobedient not only toward my parents.

In my first fifteen years of sobriety, I continued to make mistakes because of my thought process. I still held on to codependency; I still secretly held on to anger, resentment, shame, guilt, and embarrassment. I wondered how I could get back at this person or that person. How can I and when will I ever shake off my past? What I didn't realize or think about was the lack of communication, misinterpreting a word, a sentence, or even a conversation, especially with my girls' dad. Instead of me asking him why he said some of the things he said, especially pertaining to his relationships with other women and even with his past marriage, I would either retreat, try to show him that "I'm here for you," or I would even get angry. Today, before I get rubbed the wrong way, I listen and look at the situation. What does this have to do with me? Even when people drop lugs or start speaking in a different language when I enter the room, I don't take it personally, because if they have something to say to me, then they need to step up and say it to my face. I'm 5'2", 170 lbs., and in my midsixties, so I'm hardly a threat to anyone.

For example, on September 25, 2023, I was in the office scanning some documents. One of the head maintenance guys was telling the center's assistant program administrator that we're all adults and about one of the teachers who misplaced her classroom key. He went on about whether this person loses their house keys and car keys. He went on and on about if the teacher had to pay out of pocket. Now, sixteen or seventeen years ago, even in recovery, I would've taken what he said personally. The fact is, I didn't lose my work key, and I'm aware if I do lose my key, it's the wrath of his mouth I'll have to deal with. Let me just clarify for the record, his wrath is not in a disrespectful way, but he'll probably say to me, "Why would you lose your key? You need to keep it where you won't lose it. You need to be responsible"; that's what he'll say. (Plus, my coworker has a copy of my work key, so if push comes to shove, I can secretly go to her and save face.)

It was after I joined Acts Full Gospel COGIC in 2007 that I started getting into the Word through Sunday service, Bible study, and Friday Holy Ghost night. Reading the Word and what it meant, having several close friends I could talk to and pray with, I got involved with third Saturday door-to-door witnessing. Everything went back to the meetings, group/individual therapy, the workshops, and support groups, along with constantly learning about the Holy Ghost and Jesus living in my heart. Repeating the "seventh step prayer," I struggled at first with letting go of anger, shame, embarrassment, guilt, and resentment. I struggled at times with guilt and regret, but I kept holding on to God and I stayed clean. Joining the sisterhood, listening to other women speak about forgiving themselves, helped me. Combining church and my recovery, taking anger management support group, writing about what I'm going through, and going to meetings at that time, raising my hand. Looking at my lifestyle, what type of words were coming out of my mouth. Bishop would talk about "That's not a slip of the tongue, it's saying what one wants to say." James 3:5–10 KJV talks about taming my tongue. By 2012, I had to make a conscious decision: am I going to serve God or man?

Back in March 2021, as I was getting ready for work, I thought about God's grace and mercy. Having my faculties, dealing with the fact that I would have to get a left-knee replacement, yet every morning I was still able to get up and go to work. Then I thought about those who wake up in their right mind. They have their hands, feet, eyesight; they can hear and talk, but they were let go of their job. What about that woman being the sole breadwinner? (I've been down that road.) I knew what it was like to have to take my year-old Volkswagen Eurovan back to the dealership, because I could no longer pay those expensive notes, $650 per month and $450 insurance. Then in 2006, my 2003 Ford Taurus was repossessed. In 2006, after getting hired as a family advocate, as a birthday gift to myself, I purchased a brand-new 2006 Dodge Caravan. I took my past two repo experiences and turned them around for my good. I read the contract and asked a few questions before signing the contract. About three days later, a representative from Chrysler Financial called me; we renegotiated my contract, in which my notes dropped by $100. I was very pleased because I took charge; this was my money. I didn't need the dealership; they needed me. Yeeee-es.

Today, I pray and say, "Thank God for what you give me. Thank you for helping me, guiding me, and sending Your Son Jesus as my personal Lord and Savior." I tell myself, when I feel short or down or am going through something, there are those encouraging scriptures that God reminds me of: "I can do all things in Christ Jesus that strengthens me" (Philippians 4:6 KJV). For me, it means "Live the purpose God has for me, living the purpose God has for all of us." To hold on in life requires prayer, asking God, "What is it you want from me?" "Why is this happening to me?" "Father God, I can't do this without you." Instead of causing self-anxiety upon myself, giving the enemy control over me, I spend my time having faith, trust, and belief in God.

I think of so many people in my life who have mentored me, from my eighth-grade math teacher to those who pulled me aside and put that bug in my ear: don't go with that person, you should go to your mother's house or go to the shelter. Women that I had and still do admire, including those I would read about in *Ebony* magazine when I was a teenager. People were pouring into my spirit, but I didn't know it then; they were telling me not to give up, to keep moving forward, that I can be successful. My mother, who would say to me, my sisters, my children, and anyone who would listen, "Read everything you can get your hands on." Always ask the five *w*'s: who, what, where, when, and why. Then my father would always tell me, "Victoria, I know you can do it."

What would I have done without the shoulder of the executive director of Facts on Crack when I broke down and cried because I was dealing with getting visits with my daughters, or in 2010, as a family advocate at Southeast Head Start, after my workday, when I desperately needed the Word of God, knowing that evening it was Bible study that saved me from losing my mind. Could I have survived? Maybe, but not to the satisfaction where I could end my day in peace and say, "Thank you, God, I made it through this day." Knowing I survived, I did so without saying something to someone I would regret or chasing a high or getting drunk or seeking the comfort of a man, which any of these would've only magnified and made my problem worse.

I've learned to hold to scriptures: from the book of Titus, chapter 2, verses 3–4. It was a seasoned woman who helped me understand my role as a mature woman, a mother, a grandmother, and a coworker to those twenty, thirty, or thirty-five years younger than me. Having the inspiration of my family, my church family, and friends who will say, "Come on, let's pray," right when I needed it the most. Or talking on the phone to best friends who listen to me then check me or correct me, and if I get bent out of shape, they remind me, "It's life, get over it," "Move on." Even with family members, and we all know how crazy our family can be, yet without them, we can't survive; okay, I couldn't survive without my family, those who really know about me, yet they forgave me, and they love me.

What I've learned about holding on and never letting go is that I did it in the most troubled times in my life. I didn't even realize I was holding on. All I saw was the carnality, but not the spirituality. But God knew my heart, and he knew I wasn't going to give in. I didn't expect it, but it did happen. When I had that "How could that happen to me? God, where are you when I need you most? You don't do it to them, why me?" His plan for me was, is, and will always be different from others, even my family members. As long as I can see the big picture and turn away from anger, resentment, the need to get even, he always has and always will continue to provide and take care of my needs.

We're going through stuff in life, even getting resentful and angry, but stop, take that deep breath, think, and call on God. Ask yourself, "What can I do? Did I create this issue? Am I doing what I need to do?" When those voices want to war with me, keep me in confusion. The first thing is, I've got to pray and ask God for help. Then I pray for my situation and others, even those I feel like they're doing me wrong or not listening to me. For me, this is the key to forgiveness and letting go. In Jesus's mighty name. Amen, Amen, Amen.

I Am Truly Grateful

Rejoice in the Lord always: and again I say, Rejoice. Let your moderation be known unto all men. The Lord is at hand. Be careful for nothing, but in every thing by prayer and supplication with thanksgiving let your requests be made known unto God. And the peace of God, which passeth all understanding, shall keep your hearts and minds through Christ Jesus. But my God shall supply all your need according to his riches in glory by Christ Jesus.

—Philippians 4:4–7, 19 KJV

Tuesday, July 11, 2023
5:17 a.m.
Happy "Recovery" Birthday to Me: 29 Years

As I lay in bed this morning, preparing to get up and start my day, I thought about starting over in life. It's a process that starts in our early years. I thought about when the oldest child starts kindergarten, junior high, or even high school. How does one support, listen to, and advise the young person? Or as in my case, my starting over began at thirty-seven and a half. But just like with our child, as myself, praying for and with them, hugging them, letting them know that they have a place to go and talk. Most of all, teach them to go to and trust God as a major source supplier.

"For his anger endureth but a moment: in his favour is life: weeping may endure for a night, but joy cometh in the morning" (Psalm 30:5).

Up until the age of thirty-seven and a half, I settled for less. I rolled with other people's punches. As a young woman in what I see now as a dysfunctional relationship and having babies, I went through the revolving doors of poor parenting, mixed emotions and made irrational decisions, struggling through eighteen years of a turbulent and dysfunctional relationship. Turning away from God led me down a path of daily self-destruction to the ways of a wicked world that led me to drugs, alcohol, depression, cursing, bad temperament, disrespect toward my parents, separation from my children and family and community, nearly selling my soul, and near death. From 1989 to 1994, the last five years of my addiction, I lived on the streets, in shelters, sleeping on other people's couches, living room floors, and backyards/porches. In those last five years of my drug/alcohol addiction, I resorted to lying, stealing, ongoing drug-induced seizures, and cursing. It nearly cost me my sanity and my life. There were two things that kept me: (1) God kept his hands on me, even though I didn't deserve it; (2) I would have moments of hope.

In the first ten years of sobriety, I had three rental judgments against me, I accepted criticism, held resentments, got demoted from lead teacher to teacher then assistant teacher because I didn't act fast enough to reapply for my child development teacher permit, got fired from two jobs, made bad financial decisions, had two vehicle repossessions and overdrawn bank accounts, and most of all, when God would speak to me, I didn't listen, at times taking him for granted. This was mostly from 2002 to 2006; my life was a wreck, but the good news is, I never used drugs or drank alcohol, and I did have my on-call residential counseling job, which I worked an average of thirty-two hours per week, and that was a blessing. I kept going to church, attending Bible study, continued my biggest passion of singing in the choir, and most of all, I never stopped praying.

Because God saw my true worth, he had, then like now, seen purpose in me, the worth he, with the works of his hands, created in me.

"I am the true vine, and my Father is the husbandman. Abide in me, and I in you. As the branch cannot bear fruit of itself, except it abide in the vine; no more can ye, except ye abide in me. I am the vine, ye are the branches, He that abideth in me and I in him, the same bringeth forth much fruit: for without me ye can do nothing" (John 15:1–7 reference, verses 1, 4, and 5 KJV.

Fast-forward to today, after school was out on July 28, 2023, I was on a plane that night, headed to the Bay Area for two weeks. First off, I've got to say how happy and grateful I am to have my children, grandchildren, other family, and friends who love me unconditionally. I've got to tell you how I love hanging out with my four daughters; they are so special to me. God really worked with my family. When I first got clean, my son and daughters were so happy, and that gave me the strength to realize how important it was for me to be a mother. God made the way so I could start right where I was. How they always go way out for me, you know, how when you book your trip and you receive an itinerary—well, they plan an itinerary of activities whenever I'm in town.

I'm eternally grateful to God that he opened my eyes, mind, heart, and soul. When I fell to my knees asking him for help, he gave me back my life, my dignity, my self-worth, my family, and my friends. I can't explain it all; I mean, if I lived ten lifetimes at 150 years each, I still couldn't praise and thank him enough. As I prepare to transition from work to retirement, I definitely look forward to this new and exciting journey God has prepared for me. I'm taking advice I learned early in my recovery: "Take the cotton out of my ears and stuff it in my mouth." I don't know who came up with that saying, but for me, it's a great learning and "I can live with" tool.

I'm also grateful to God because, even in my pitfalls, all the mistakes I made in life, the struggles I went through, God kept that door open, so when I got clean, I got the chance to rededicate my life to him by going back to my spiritual roots. Taking those baby steps, starting with Glide Sunday service, then Our Lady of Lourdes from 1995 to 2006, where I began to grow as a reader and choir member. In late 2006, there was a huge spiritual step: I left the Catholic church but on good terms to begin new members' class at Acts Full Gospel

COGIC, along with Chizon classes and getting full water baptized. It was at Acts where I really grew spiritually in many areas of my life. Learning the importance of prayer on a group as well as individually. Joining other ministries, third Saturday door-to-door witnessing, and attending church business meetings. It was here where God poured into my spirit because what I did at Acts was useful in my daily life. I was a part of the youth ministry, and most of all, I brought my grandchildren regularly where they attended Sunday school, youth service, and vacation Bible school. Two of my daughters attend Acts. My oldest and third daughters are still practicing Catholics.

In July 2015, while visiting Michael in Brooklyn, while walking the neighborhood, I found and started attending Mount Moriah COGIC. I would attend anytime I was in town, and once I moved here, I attended regularly. During that time, my coworker had a bring-a-friend-to-church event at the Church of the First Born at Utica and Church here in Brooklyn. I would attend off and on. But I ended up visiting Mount Sinai Cathedral COGIC, where I joined the church in 2018, and in early 2019, I completed my new members' class. I've been a member since. I tell you, there are songs that sing those lines: "Never give up on God because he is always on standby waiting for each and every one of us, even the worst of the worst." There is no sin that he won't forgive; that's why he gave his Son Jesus as a living sacrifice so we can have eternal life. We see it in the Bible with Paul when he was Saul of Tarsus, a Christian tormentor and killer if necessary.

Acts Full Gospel Church Of God In Christ
Bishop Bob Jackson, Pastor
1034 66th Avenue Oakland, CA 94621
(510) 567-1300 . (510) 568-4125 FAX
The Five Steps of Christian Growth
NEW MEMBERS WORK BOOK
HOLY BIBLE
Student's Name Victoria Stith
Teacher's Name Sr Gloria Mothershed
Date Oct 22, 2006 to
"Study to show thy self approve unto God a workman that needed not be ashamed rightly dividing the Word of God." 2 Timothy 2:15

Certificate of Church Membership
This Certifies That
Victoria Jude Pearl Stith
1811 27th Avenue Apt 213
Oakland, California
has publicly confessed the Lord Jesus Christ as her Lord and Saviour
and has been received into the full membership of
Acts Full Gospel Church of God in Christ
1034 66th Avenue
Oakland, California
on the 31st day of December in the year of our Lord 2006
February 7, 2007
Date
Bishop Bob Jackson, Pastor
The Lord added to the church daily such as should be saved. Acts 2:47
Teacher: Gloria Mothershed

Certificate of Baptism
This Certifies That
Victoria Jude Pearl Stith
1811 27th Avenue Apt 213
Oakland, California
born on November 22, 1956 in St. Louis, Missouri
was baptized
in the name of the Father and of the Son and of the Holy Ghost
on the 4th day of February in the year of our Lord 2007
at Acts Full Gospel Church of God in Christ,
1034 66th Avenue Oakland, California
Bishop Bob Jackson, Pastor
Go ye therefore, and teach all nations, baptizing them in
the name of the Father, and of the Son and of the Holy Ghost. Matthew 28:19

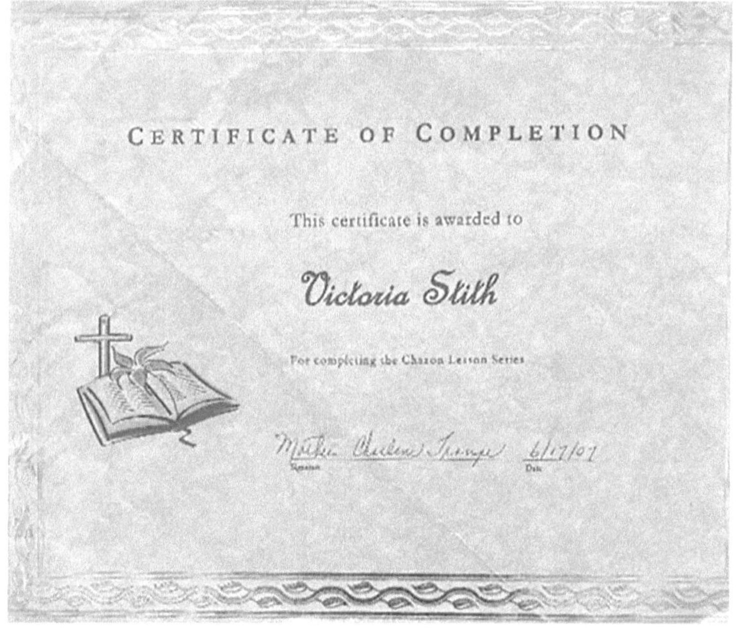

CERTIFICATE OF COMPLETION
This certificate is awarded to
Victoria Stith
For completing the Chazon Lesson Series

MT. SINAI CATHEDRAL CHURCH OF GOD IN CHRIST

CERTIFICATE OF GRADUATION

Awarded To

Victoria Stith

In completion of the New Members/New Convert Class at
Mt. Sinai Cathedral Church of God in Christ
1916 Fulton Street, Brooklyn, New York 11233

For your cooperation, participation and faithfulness
Presented this Twenty-Fourth Day of March, 2019

Missionary Elizabeth Elcock
Instructor

Bishop Clarence L. Sexton, Jr.
Pastor

CERTIFICATE

OF APPRECIATION

IS PRESENTED TO

Victoria Stith

In honor of Women's History Month, we celebrate your
accomplishments and your contributions towards your
church and community.

Mountain Youth Ministries   Bishop Clarence L. Sexton, Jr. Pastor

Growing up in church, there were belief systems that Christian denominations had. Growing up Catholic, as a teenager, I would be told at times by my mother, "Good Catholic girls don't do such things." Let me share one of her sneak attacks. I was about seventeen at the time, and I went out with several friends on a late night, washing my sweater at midnight. As I would reluctantly take my sweater off, she would grab it and start going through my pockets. She would find a weed butt, loose tobacco, and half a book of matches. That's when those sayings came: "You know what *Victoria* means? It means *victorious*." I would see my peers at church with their mothers and fathers; everyone sat together, they dressed in their Sunday attire, they seemed so together. Or the "sanctified kids" at school stuck together—they stood out; they were the "good" kids. Or there were the "holy rollers." When they talked, nothing but scriptures came out of their mouths. I tell you, at times I would feel awkward because, first off, nothing I responded to these holy rollers with was correct or met their "godly standards," and usually, these were people who had skeletons in their closets, or their families were in disarray. What I learned after renewing my life with Christ Jesus is that ignorance can follow me in my attempt to live godly and holy, because was I living for God or to look like I'm doing the right thing before others? Which is the scripture Hosea 4:6—"It's our lack of knowledge," our refusal to accept change, see the bigger picture, look at what and why people are in their family situations. This is what can keep me separated from God and miss out on the blessings (Malachi 3:8–12), because, like my past, I could continually keep living outside myself, not really ever getting it because I'm trying to please man (which will never happen due to man's jealousy, criticism, and always seeing the wrong and the fact that we're all born in sin). "We cannot serve man and mammon. We must love one and hate the other" (Matthew 6:24 KJV). I'm constantly learning, and at times, I feel challenged. He's given me direction and purpose in life, a real reason to live. God took my dreams and turned them into reality, such as going back to college, earning an associate of arts and bachelor's degrees. Now I live in Brooklyn, New York; I have friends who don't laugh at me behind my back. My friends love me unconditionally; they don't always agree with me, but they give me advice. My friends pray for me and with me.

What God did for me was, he took my sins, misconceptions, mistakes, and misunderstandings and turned them into testimonies. I can look back and be able to share with my grandchildren to let them know they don't have to walk down the negative wide roads of life. They have and will have their storms, trials, tribulations, and even temptations in life, but teaching and having taught them about God, Jesus Christ, and the Holy Ghost, they have choices, and at times when they may consider the easy sinful way out, I pray for them that their Christian upbringing will kick in, give them the strength and wisdom to say no to the adversary. In closing, I thank you, God, for the grace, mercy, and protection you have shown and continue to show toward me. I will love you always and forevermore. Your loving daughter, Vickie.

> Rejoice evermore. Pray without ceasing. In every thing give thanks: for this is the will of God in Christ Jesus concerning you. Quench not the Spirit. Despise not prophesyings. Prove all things; hold fast that which is good. Abstain from all appearance of evil. And the very God of peace sanctify you wholly; and I pray God your whole spirit and soul and body be preserved blameless unto the coming of our Lord Jesus Christ. Faithful is he that calleth you, who also will do it. Brethren, pray for us. Greet all the brethren with a holy kiss. I charge you by the Lord that this epistle be read unto all the holy brethren. The grace of our Lord Jesus Christ be with you. Amen. (1 Thessalonians 5:16–28 KJV)

Epilogue

Therefore also now, saith the Lord turn ye
even to me with all your heart, and with fasting,
and with weeping and with mourning.

—Joel 2:12

My Help Cometh is a gripping testimonial of how God answers prayer. It illustrates how he can turn one's life around with his promises and help. Anyone can emerge from the mess they have made of their life by crying out to God, asking for help, and then receiving the opportunity to give a gripping testimony of what God can and will do. Whether you are going through the loss of a job that leaves you struggling, issues in your marriage, or challenges with your child or children going astray, or it can be you—God can and will help. You just have to call on him and mean it from the bottom of your heart.

Because of the promise I made to God in 1994, even in my mistakes after I stopped using drugs and alcohol, I learned a crucial lesson. Although drugs and alcohol were no longer an option or consideration for me, I replaced them with complacency. I took God for granted by doing things my way. I became ungrateful for all he had done for me, yet at the same time, I kept praying, going to church, singing in the choir, and crying and pleading to God until I got it right. I was taught that Jesus living in my heart and the Holy Ghost abiding in me helps me today to make rational and sane decisions.

My Help Cometh only proves that God showing up in my life in his time is a confirmation that God is not done with me yet. God bless you, and thank you for taking the time to read this book. I pray that this book will be your confirmation to not give up on life, not give up on that loved one who's struggling, and please, whatever you do, hold on to your faith in God. Always remember, don't give up on him because he will come through for you.

> That if thou shalt confess with thy mouth the Lord Jesus, and shalt believe in thine heart that God hath raised Him from the dead, thou shalt be saved. (Romans 10:9)

Love always,
Victoria Stith

About the Author

After writing her first book, *Who Am I, Am I*, Victoria Stith was inspired by the Holy Spirit to write *My Help Cometh*. This was quite a project because her feelings of shame, guilt, and concerns about what people would think about her surfaced. After praying to God for courage, it was revealed to Victoria that this is not just a story but a gripping testimonial of her life and life's experiences.

Along Victoria's journey, she had to learn, and is still learning, how to walk into the unknown yet fully trust in God, staying determined to walk on the straight road of life.

Today, when she looks in the mirror, Victoria sees a woman who is precious in the eyes of God. And that is what keeps her motivated. By sharing her story, Victoria wants the world to know that no matter how dark and cloudy life may seem, the light of God can and will burst through if you let him. Thank you, and God bless you.